Mythology and Humanism

THE CORRESPONDENCE OF
THOMAS MANN AND
KARL KERÉNYI

Mythology and Humanism

THE CORRESPONDENCE OF THOMAS MANN AND KARL KERÉNYI

Translated from the German by
ALEXANDER GELLEY

Cornell University Press | ITHACA AND LONDON

First published 1975 by Cornell University Press.
Published in the United Kingdom by Cornell University Press Ltd., 2-4 Brook Street, London W1Y 1AA.

Cornell University Press gratefully acknowledges a grant from the Andrew J. Mellon Foundation that aided in bringing this book to publication.

International Standard Book Number 0-8014-0831-8
Library of Congress Catalog Card Number 73-20796

Printed in the United States of America by York Composition Co., Inc.

Contents

42390

Translator's Preface

Among the private documents that have become available in recent years, Thomas Mann's correspondence may appear as an anomaly. It is exceptionally voluminous,[1] yet it does not offer the kind of intimate, unguarded revelations that many contemporary readers expect to find in an artist's letters. The exchanges with certain friends and family members reveal considerable warmth and intensity of contact, as in the letters to his brother Heinrich or those to the friend of his middle years Ernst Bertram.[2] But the majority of Mann's published letters could well be classified as a form of public intellectual discourse rather than as private communications.

Mann was capable of voicing some of his most pressing intellectual and personal concerns to individuals who were not particularly close to him. For Mann personal issues usually involved an inseparable public dimension. This may be partly accounted for by his background and temperament. His fame came early, and in the course of his life Mann developed a

1. It has been estimated that Mann wrote between twelve thousand and fifteen thousand letters in his lifetime. The largest single collection, that of the Mann archives in Zurich, comprises about thirty-two hundred. See Reinhold Grimm's review of four volumes of Mann letters, including the exchange with Kerényi, in *Germanisch-Romanische Monatsschrift,* 43 (1962), 428–432.

2. Thomas Mann and Heinrich Mann, *Briefwechsel: 1900–1949* (Frankfort on the Main, 1968); *Thomas Mann an Ernst Bertram: Briefe aus den Jahren 1910–1955* (Pfullingen, 1960).

public posture which became virtually second nature. It was a complex posture, which included but also transcended the level of an assumed role, an imposture. (The very ambiguity implicit in the artist's public role was, of course, a persistent theme in his fiction.) Yet, while fully imbued with the modern artist's sense of self-doubt, Mann was also the heir of an older, a bourgeois, predisposition to consider the artist as a representative and spokesman of his age. He did not shirk this function, even though the radical disorientation of European public life after the First World War made it more precarious than in the previous generation. Thus what was "personal" for Mann was not limited by the sphere of private concerns but extended to the compelling historical and cultural issues of his age.

Just as Mann welcomed the opportunity to appear in public —to lecture, to read from his works, even to participate in purely ceremonial occasions—so he responded with readiness and warmth to many correspondents whom he knew slightly or not at all. What motivated him was first of all a sense of what he owed to his public position. Already in 1916 he wrote to a friend that he had "long been used to attending to [the correspondence], both conscientiously and considerately, as part of [his] duties as a public person."[3] But this sense of duty cannot by itself account for the energy and commitment that are reflected in so many of the letters. One often finds in them echoes of the work in progress. Mann seems to have relished the opportunity to pursue his thinking on the subject that possessed him beyond the confines of the work itself.[4] Finally, the correspondence reflects Mann's receptivity to new facts and ideas. He had an absorbing interest in a variety of subjects, and he knew well how to channel it to furthering "the task at

3. *Letters to Paul Amann* (Middletown, Conn., 1960), p. 78 (originally published in Lübeck, 1959).

4. See, for example, Mann to Kerényi, December 5, 1954, below, which reflects Mann's preparations for his *Versuch über Schiller*.

hand."[5] The letters reveal how readily, though discriminatingly, he drew on the stimulation and the information provided by others.

This receptivity, which should neither be ignored nor exaggerated, was a basic constituent of his nature as a writer. In an early letter we find "I say that very great writers have throughout their lives invented nothing [*nichts erfunden*], but only used what has been transmitted, infusing it with their spirit and giving it new form."[6] Forty-three years later, in *The Story of a Novel: The Genesis of Doctor Faustus*, Mann characterized his "montage technique" as a "ruthless process of structuring and amalgamating [*Aufmontieren*] factual, historical, personal, even literary data, in such a way . . . that palpable reality was forever indistinguishably merging into perspectual simulations and illusions."[7] Although each of these statements represents a specific stage in a long and differentiated process of development, they serve to indicate the dependence of Mann's creative activity on external data. And such data were characteristically derived more from the reading of secondary materials and from expert informants than from the study of original sources or from direct observation.

Recent studies that have utilized Mann's working notes and his library have begun to disclose the enormous range of specialized information incorporated into his fiction, information drawn from scholarly and popular works, from histories, memoirs, and diaries, from religious and mythological narratives.[8] Mann made no effort to conceal his borrowings, but he

5. See Mann to Kerényi, July 18, 1946, below.

6. Mann to Kurt Martens, March 28, 1906, in Thomas Mann, *Briefe, 1889–1936*, ed. Erika Mann (Frankfort on the Main, 1961), p. 62.

7. This translation is adapted from the English edition (New York, 1961), p. 32 (*Die Entstehung des Doktor Faustus* [Amsterdam, 1949]; *GW*, XI, 165).

8. See especially the two volumes of Thomas-Mann-Studien that have appeared so far under the sponsorship of the Mann archives,

also felt no obligation to document them, feeling that the artistic structure effectively submerged and transformed whatever alien elements went into it. The task of salvaging these elements—whether factual data, concepts, or narrative segments—and of incorporating them into a new totality engaged his creative powers no less fully than the process of free invention. In a letter on the sources of *The Holy Sinner* he wrote, not altogether playfully, "A secret magnetism very often brings me books [required for the work at hand] precisely at the right moment." And in the same letter he put in the form of a pun a justification for his predaceous practice: "Thus what is found [*Gefundene*] becomes in a certain sense something invented [*Erfundene*]."[9]

Karl Kerényi inaugurated the contact with Mann in 1934 by sending him the offprint of an article on an aspect of Greek religion. Kerényi, at thirty-six, had just attained a professorship in his native Hungary, while Mann was nearly sixty and at the height of his fame. (Mann was also, it should be added, beginning the second year of his self-exile from Germany, a step necessitated by the Nazi assumption of power in 1933.) Mann's warm acknowledgment marked the beginning of an exchange that was to last over twenty years, until his death in 1955. The two met for the first time in January 1935, when Mann went to Budapest for a lecture, and met regularly though not frequently in subsequent years. Kerényi sent many of his publications to Mann over the years, and it is clear from the letters that Mann found them not only of interest but often of real use for his work. The correspondence of the two grew into an ongoing commentary on work in progress, and its par-

Zurich: Paul Scherrer and Hans Wysling, *Quellenkritische Studien zum Werk Thomas Manns* (Bern and Munich, 1967); and Manfred Dierks, *Studien zu Mythos und Psychologie bei Thomas Mann* (Bern and Munich, 1972).

9. Mann to Erich Auerbach (*GW*, XI, 693).

ticular value for students of Mann lies in the illumination it provides for his later work, both through his own words and through those of an alert and erudite admirer.

Kerényi's own development had turned him from the historical and positivist methods of classical philology, typified by the work of Ulrich Wilamowitz-Moellendorff, toward a more anthropologically oriented approach to the religious and mythological traditions of antiquity, one inspired by such Romantic thinkers as Johann Jakob Bachofen, to whom Mann also responded favorably.[10] The initial contact came at a propitious moment for Mann, who was then embarked on his first avowedly "mythical" undertaking, the tetralogy *Joseph and His Brothers*. This work, begun in the middle 1920's and not completed until 1943, marked a decisive juncture in his artistic evolution. Mann himself summed up the achievement of the Joseph novels in the following words:

It is probably a rule that at a certain age one gradually loses the taste for everything that is merely individual and particular, for the single instance, for the "bourgeois" in the large sense of the word. Instead the focus of interest shifts toward the typical, the eternally human, eternally recurrent, ageless, in short: the mythical. For the typical is already the mythical insofar as it is a primordial norm and primordial form of life, a timeless schema and ever-present formula into which the life process enters as it reproduces its own features from out of the unconscious. Unquestionably, the attainment of a mythic-typical viewpoint marked an epoch in the life of the writer [i.e., of Mann himself], it signified a singular intensification of his artistic mood, a new gaiety and vividness of both his cognitive and his formative powers which, as stated, seems to be reserved for riper years. For while the mythical represents an early and primitive form in the life of mankind, in that of the individual it is a late and ripe one.[11]

10. See Mann to Kerényi, December 3, 1945, below.
11. From a lecture on *Joseph and His Brothers* (*GW*, XI, 656).

This passage, written in 1942, reflects the culmination of a development that Mann underwent during the 1930's.[12] The first part of the Mann-Kerényi correspondence is one of the primary sources for tracing this development. Kerényi's introduction to the German editions of the correspondence, translated below, provides a discussion of other major themes of the letters.

The intellectual curiosity and wide-ranging learning that made Kerényi so stimulating a correspondent for Mann are reflected in his own career. Kerényi was born in Temesvár, Hungary, in 1897 and died in Zurich on April 14, 1973. After studying classical philology in Budapest and at a number of German universities, notably Greifswald and Heidelberg, he began his academic career as a docent in Budapest in 1927. In that year his first major book appeared, in German, like most of his writings: *Die griechisch-orientalische Romanliteratur in religionsgeschichtlicher Beleuchtung* ("Greek-Oriental Fiction from a Religious-Historical Perspective"). Kerényi attained a professorship in 1934, first at Pécs and then at Szeged, but he felt compelled to leave Hungary in 1943 in consequence of his country's effective subordination by Nazi Germany. He settled in the Italian part of Switzerland, Tessin (Ticino), which became his home for the rest of his life. Kerényi held no regular academic appointment during this period, though he served on occasion as a guest professor, notably in Basel and Bonn and in the theological faculty of the University of Zurich. From 1941

12. Mann's view represents, of course, a self-interpretation after the fact. It is possible to explain the genesis of *Joseph and His Brothers* in quite different terms—for example, Herbert Lehnert sees it as a response to political and cultural currents of the twenties, in his "Fictional Orientations in Thomas Mann's Biography," *Publications of the Modern Language Association of America,* 88 (1973), 1146–1161, especially 1148 f.

on, a number of his studies on mythology were published together with commentaries by the psychoanalyst Carl Gustav Jung. Kerényi became one of the founders of the C. G. Jung Institute in Zurich and was a regular lecturer there from 1948 until 1962. He published some thirty books, in addition to numerous essays, on classical and modern literature, archaeology, psychology, the history of mythology and religion, as well as travel impressions growing out of his frequent and extensive journeys to the sites of Greek and Roman antiquities. Although Kerényi continued his specialized scholarly studies during his Swiss period, many of his works of that time were directed toward a general reading public. A number of his books have been translated into English and other languages.

Part I of this correspondence, edited by Kerényi, was originally published in 1945 under the title *Romandichtung und Mythologie,* Albae Vigiliae series, N.S. I (Zurich: Rhein-Verlag). Mann's letters from Part I, with minor abridgments, were included by him in the volume *Altes und Neues* (Frankfort on the Main, 1953), as a commentary on his own work (also in *GW,* XI, 629–653). Part II comprises the letters that were exchanged from 1945 until Mann's death in 1955. In 1960, Kerényi published both parts (with certain passages restored that had been omitted in the first edition of Part I) under the title *Gespräch in Briefen* ("Dialogue in Letters"; Zurich: Rhein-Verlag). Part II is titled "Humanismus—schweres Glück," while Part I retains the title under which it was first published. For this translation of the 1960 edition the part titles have been translated, but the whole volume has been given a new title that reflects the principal concerns of the writers in these letters.

The ellipses within brackets are also in the German edition and presumably indicate deletions by Kerényi or by Mann.

[xiii]

The unbracketed sets of three dots reproduce punctuation in that edition.

The notes include those prepared by Kerényi for the 1960 edition; bibliographical references have been checked, updated, and amplified. The translator has also provided additional notes, indicated by bracketed numbers.

Of the many individuals who have advised him on various aspects of this work, he wishes particularly to thank Dr. Barbara K. Gold, who traced and translated most of the classical citations, and Dr. Herbert Lehnert, who provided information on a number of matters relating to Mann.

ALEXANDER GELLEY

Irvine, California

Abbreviations

ASM *Auf Spuren des Mythos.* Vol. II of Karl Kerényi, *Werke in Einzelausgaben.* Munich and Vienna, 1967.

GW Thomas Mann. *Gesammelte Werke.* 12 vols. Frankfort on the Main, 1960.

HSF *Humanistische Seelenforschung.* Vol. I of Karl Kerényi, *Werke in Einzelausgaben.* Munich and Vienna, 1966.

Mythology and Humanism

THE CORRESPONDENCE OF THOMAS MANN AND KARL KERÉNYI

To the young intellectuals who suffered in the war and were left unsatisfied after it

"These fragments of two autobiographies communicatively intertwined"

T. M.

Foreword

This volume contains the entire dialogue in letters that I was permitted to hold with Thomas Mann from January 27, 1934, until his death—with a single, enormous interruption, from September 7, 1941, to December 21, 1944. I had already gathered the first part of the correspondence, up to the great caesura, and, together with an introduction, had made a small book of it in 1944, utilizing the original letters of Thomas Mann and my own drafts, so that, whatever might ensue, a document in the history of humanism in Europe might remain. At the beginning of 1945, Thomas Mann was able to read and correct the prepared text. Today, after a much greater interval, it is also possible to print certain things that we omitted at the time. With astonishing speed, what is discussed in the second part of the dialogue—comprising almost twice as many letters as the first—has already become part of "history." I called the first part "Mythology and the Making of a Novel." So that the second part may also have a title, I call it "Humanism—Painful Destiny."

For the collation of Thomas Mann's letters, of which I possess the originals, I am deeply grateful to Dr. Paul Scherrer, Director of the Thomas Mann Archives in Zurich.

K. K.

Ascona
February 3, 1960

Introduction

by Karl Kerényi

Andros, September 1959—Ascona, February 1960

For my stay on the island of Andros [Greece] I took along copies of the letters that were still to come out, together with the published first part of the correspondence; by 1955 the collection had already attained its definitive form. I was asked even then to publish the second part of the correspondence. But at the time, after the death of Thomas Mann, I initially sought refuge in copying the letters, in occupying myself with them, in evoking the ten years since the appearance of the first half of the dialogue, years full of disappointments but also rich in blessings, and rich particularly because of the dialogue that could still be continued. For me, that dialogue had been a kind of refuge. Now at least I could go to an island refuge, a remote real island, in order to evoke, to meditate on, the relationship these letters document. The island, furthermore, held certain secrets for me, secrets that were to disclose themselves beyond my expectations. It was under these circumstances that I composed this part of the introduction; I place it here before those earlier reflections which originated near Lake Maggiore between Ascona and Arcegno and which served to introduce the first part of the correspondence.

I could not help recalling a famous discovery, the Hermes of Andros, made on the island in the previous century, although that god was not the object of my own search there. I felt a correspondence between the gentle coloring of the statue, its almost opaque shimmer, and that special emanation or aura (one can describe it only figuratively, through sense impressions) that enchanted me during my first, significant reading of one of Thomas Mann's novels. I wished not merely to convey to the readers of the letters the nature of my enchantment, but also to test it, as it were, in the atmosphere: to determine whether this elusive substance could really survive under the Greek sky—a substance that I had once called the "higher reality" of Hermes and that, it seemed to me, was only in a secondary sense *depicted* in *The Magic Mountain* [1924][1] but was in a primary sense *operative* within it. In my first letter to Thomas Mann I spoke of such "realities" as so self-evident that I felt it best to omit the whole passage when publishing the first part of the correspondence, for fear of giving rise to misapprehensions, which at the time were all too likely to arise. Thomas Mann showed that he understood me. On February 20, 1934, he wrote, "That 'return of the European spirit to the highest, the mythic realities' of which you speak so impressively is in truth a great and positive cultural movement, and I may claim that my own work has to some extent played a part in it." These words represented a singular confirmation for me: they came from an opponent of the irrationalists. The foundation for our intellectual relationship was thus established. This foundation became the object of my meditations in Andros, and I think I was not mistaken in seeing in Thomas Mann an embodiment of that "Hermetic" spirit that the inhabitants of the island had worshiped along with various other manifestations of the divine.

What gave me the idea at the beginning of 1934 of sending my lecture "Unsterblichkeit und Apollonreligion" (delivered in the spring of 1933 at the Hungarian Philosophical Society

[1.] Throughout the text the English titles of Mann's works are given, but the dates in brackets refer to the first German editions.

[6]

in Budapest and then translated into German for the periodical *Die Antike*)[2] to Thomas Mann? It was the portrait of a god made of light and darkness, although, it seemed to me, of a clearer light and a deeper opacity than the Hermes figure that emerged from *The Magic Mountain*. For me the critical experience in reading Thomas Mann did not come, for example, from *Buddenbrooks* but, soon after the appearance of the Hungarian translation in 1925 or 1926, from *The Magic Mountain*. It was primarily this novel to which I referred in the dedication I wrote for the published version of the lecture: "To the great writer who has given us the figure of Settembrini, and to one of the most profound historians of religion."

In the figure of Settembrini[3] Thomas Mann realized what was for me an exceptionally sympathetic embodiment of the humanistic spirit confronting an eternally recurrent human situation, one which on the level of scholarship is part of the field of the history of religion. I mean the situation of closeness to death and the resultant attitudes toward death itself. The fundamental proximity of human existence and death, in fact the very conjunction of the two, proved to be a dimension of *The Magic Mountain* in which Thomas Mann moved with more assurance, acuity, and precision (and this "movement" refers also to his control of the expressive power of language) than any scholar who had ever ventured into it. He moved in this realm of human existence, this border area between life and death, as the Greeks believed their god Hermes did. The spiritual reality of the god Hermes, the basis of the faith he once inspired, involved a capability that, after all, also corresponds to an exceptional capacity of the mind: to be at home even in that realm.

To perceive realms of human existence in their dominant figures, to enter into these figures, to make them vivid by

[2.] See Mann to Kerényi, January 27, 1934, note 1.
[3.] A character in *The Magic Mountain*.

means of language, but to do this particularly for one or another such figure who at the same time represents the observer's own essential nature—this seemed to me a triumph of intellect that the field of classical scholarship, and not only this field but any discipline devoted to a period of man's history in which the "mythic realities" ("realities" in the sense just discussed) were active, should strive to emulate. It should do so at least by utilizing the method of phenomenological description, of a form of interpretation directed to the nature of man and his potentialities. Such was the conclusion I came to in those years. And this is why I paid homage to Thomas Mann by sending him my lecture and why I wrote him in my first letter: "Both your Joseph novel and Powys' *Glastonbury Romance* testify to the return of the European spirit to the highest, the mythic realities. In comparison, the field of scholarship certainly lags behind."[4]

I had possessed *The Tales of Jacob* [1933][5] as early as 1933; and although, unlike the following volumes, the book did not come from him, it was still a gift from a dear friend. In my dedication I meant to refer also to the beginnings of that mythological novel. But my concern with the "Hermetic" in Thomas Mann—an ever-growing concern on my part—was expressed clearly enough in my gratulatory message on his sixtieth birthday (published for the first time in the present volume),[6] which was part of the presentation that the Fischer Verlag made to him on that occasion. I allowed myself there a consciously stilted, humanistically archaic tone, legitimized by the ceremonial occasion, to celebrate him in his guise of

[4.] The passage here is slightly different from that in the letter of February 7 (?), 1934.

[5.] The first volume of the tetralogy *Joseph and His Brothers*. The others are *Young Joseph* (1934), *Joseph in Egypt* (1936), and *Joseph the Provider* (1943).

[6.] See Mann to Kerényi, September 6, 1935, note 2.

Doctor Hermeticus, whose work and nature are a revelation of the god. In this manner I could express my view of the nature of the "Hermetic" as well as of Thomas Mann himself. Today, looking back at our exchange, I do not think I exaggerate when I say that the dominance in European cultural history of the dualism of Apollonian and Dionysian introduced by Nietzsche was first broken by our letters, on the publication of the first part. The Hermetic was thus added as a third element, "Hermetic" to be understood in terms of mythological antiquity and not in the Gnostic or alchemical sense, much less as a movement of modern poetry.

Naturally, if one focuses only on those forms and stylistic patterns in Thomas Mann that are consciously modeled on antiquity, or on those figures who are expressly identified as Hermes or Hermes-like, then one remains far from any decisive understanding—namely, the understanding of a specific quality in the nature, achievements, and life patterns of mankind, as well as of the corresponding traits of roguery to be found on the surface of man's world. There is a rudimentary philological method—one may call it childish in comparison with the methods of the more serious scholarly disciplines of today—well exemplified by such an intentionally simplifying title as "Der Gott der Diebe und sein Dichter" ["The God of Thieves and His Poet"].[7] It is as unsuitable in this case as it would be in an analysis of Hofmannsthal's relation to the Greeks.[8] Both writers—Thomas Mann unintentionally, Hofmannsthal through dedicated effort—have enabled us to increase our receptivity to the spiritual reality of antiquity. The field of classical scholarship cannot afford to ignore such a growth of

[7.] The title of a chapter on Mann and the world of antiquity in Walter Jens's *Statt einer Literaturgeschichte* (Pfullingen, 1957).

[8.] Hugo von Hofmannsthal (1874–1929), Austrian poet and dramatist. A number of his plays and opera libretti are based on Greek mythological subjects, e.g., *Alkestis, Ariadne auf Naxos, Elektra.*

awareness—that is, unless it acquiesces altogether in the disintegration which has overtaken it on all sides since the Second World War, a disintegration into an authoritarian establishment without major sources of authority, characterized by a gradual loss of scholarly quality and by a notable inhumanity. (Such was not yet the case in the time of Ulrich von Wilamowitz-Moellendorff, who is criticized in these letters.)

Faithful to the roguish disposition of the great Hermetic master, I leave the source-hunting to others; let them uncover whatever has found its way from my writings into that great narrative art which has been for me a blissful addiction to the very end, to the last lines of *Krull* [*Confessions of Felix Krull, Confidence Man: The Early Years,* 1954], and whose silencing cuts me off from a source of the sublimest joy. Our relationship has been viewed in a somewhat oversimplified fashion even by such a serious scholar as Bengt Algot Sörensen in his study on *Doctor Faustus* (*Orbis Litterarum,* 1958).[9] Leaving aside the question whether or to what extent the basic conception of the novel was already enunciated in the letter I wrote on August 13, 1934, from a Dalmatian island, I do not believe that my impressions of Germany at the time played any significant role in the genesis of *Doctor Faustus.* And I was certainly not, in the accepted sense of the word, "Mann's *expert* in matters of myth." When, among other plans, he considered an Achilles novel, a continuation of Goethe's *Achilleis,* he played with the idea of seeking my advice, for I was then occupied with my *Heroen der Griechen.*[10] But he never actually did so, and he required no "expert in matters of myth."

[9.] "Thomas Manns *Doktor Faustus,* Mythos und Lebensbeichte," *Orbis Litterarum,* 13 (1958), 81–97. It is here that Kerényi is referred to as "Mann's expert in matters of myth" (p. 85).

[10.] Zurich, 1958 (*The Heroes of the Greeks,* trans. H. J. Rose, [London, 1959]). On the Achilles novel see Mann to Kerényi, March 20, 1952.

He himself read, and he took in and assimilated what corresponded to his entelechy. I sent him my work, including offprints of specialized philological essays and reviews. I could never know in advance to what he would respond. But I had the strongest confidence in his entelechy and its mythological inclination—perhaps even stronger than his own.

In using the word "entelechy" to identify that in Thomas Mann in which I placed my fullest confidence and with which I believe I stood in closest contact during all the years of our acquaintance, I do so in the hope that perhaps by drawing on certain passages from the conversations of Goethe with Eckermann I may make this elusive topic more comprehensible. On March 3, 1830, Goethe said of the entelechy: "The obstinancy of the individual, and the fact that man shakes off what is not proper to him, are proof for me that something like that exists." And on March 11, 1828: "If the entelechy is of a powerful sort, as is the case with all whose nature is akin to genius, then, in its vital penetration of the body, it will not only strengthen and ennoble the corporeal structure, but also, through its spiritual dominance, continually seek to assert its right to an eternal youth. That is why we may see in highly gifted individuals ever renewed periods of unusual productivity, even into old age; they seem to undergo a temporary rejuvenation over and over again, and it is this that I would call a recurrent puberty."[11]

In his first letter to me, Thomas Mann wrote that his interest in the history of religion and in mythology had been a product of his mature years and was not at all present in youth. In this he seemed to stand close to the aged Aristotle (Fr. 668, Rose), as an English reviewer of my *Mythologie der Griechen*[12] re-

[11.] Johann Peter Eckermann, *Gespräche mit Goethe in den letzten Jahren seines Lebens,* ed. H. H. Houben (Wiesbaden, 1959), pp. 304, 513.

[12.] Zurich, 1951 (*The Gods of the Greeks,* trans. N. Cameron [London, 1951]).

marked. But undoubtedly the Greek philosopher had found pleasure in myths in his youth, and it must have been the same with Thomas Mann. His was an entelechy of many marvels of rejuvenation, from the first volume of the Joseph novel to his final, interrupted effort to complete the fragment of *Krull;* and he bore witness to its deeply buried levels, its potent roots when he wrote to me on September 23, 1951, "Am reading the *Mythologie* like a boy," and again, on March 20, 1952, when he confessed that as he read it he always had to think of the old book of mythological tales his mother had used for his instruction and in which he read insatiably as a child. After sixty-seven years he could recall whole sentences from it, and he was convinced that the same words would still occur to him in his dying hour. Thus an arc that connected beginning and end was reconstituted before my eyes—can I possibly express how great was my response and emotion?

A great entelechy with mythological inclinations, indeed with a mythological disposition that may be considered a fundamental gestalt, together with the roguish traits of a Hermetic nature: this is how I see Thomas Mann when all transient, familiar, social, ephemeral elements are shaken off— which, however, he did not do in his own life, for he was one of those exceptional types who are able to meet the demands of both the inner *and* the outer self. He succeeded in this, but not without unresolved tensions nor with an always balanced disposition of his powers. And here I reach a point where I must cite the words of Wilhelm von Humboldt, words that would have served as a motto for my essay on *Doctor Faustus* if I could have brought myself to write one. On January 6, 1832, Humboldt wrote to Goethe, "It is the strangest experience to be called upon to dissect in public, as it were, a singular individual for whom one feels all possible veneration and love."[13] I cannot now avoid speaking of *Doctor Faustus* too,

[13.] *Briefe an Goethe,* ed. Karl Robert Mandelkow (Hamburg, 1969), II, 608.

of the secret of the work, which is barely touched on in our dialogue. The allusions in my letters need to be explained.

I shall simplify considerably, but I believe that in this way I can most easily keep at a distance the intimate, merely personal biographical element—which certainly also has its charm in Thomas Mann—and put in the foreground the great human qualities. I shall keep the term borrowed from Goethe without necessarily adopting his views on the subject. A great literary entelechy enters into innumerable figures: often unwillingly, dividing itself or flirting with possibilities that also existed in itself. Models are chosen from other entelechies that have achieved complete realization, as Gerhart Hauptmann was for Mijnheer Peeperkorn.[14] I like to think that in working on *The Magic Mountain,* Thomas Mann, with his southern maternal inheritance, identified principally with the dark-eyed Signor Settembrini. But he always lets one feel a certain distance from him—specifically, what a Hanseatic patrician's son might feel about an Italian organ grinder. And then there was also Naphta, an astonishing product of his montage technique, as Thomas Mann himself called it. With the prophetic eye of genius he perceived the infernal spirit in the dogmatist. (I would rather not name the model here.) And finally, there is also Hans Castorp, an almost Hermetic but still indeterminate entelechy.[15]

[14.] Gerhart Hauptmann (1862–1946), the German dramatist, served as a model for the figure of Pieter Peeperkorn in *The Magic Mountain.* Mann's own views on this instance of a characterization drawn from life are well documented in letters he wrote shortly after the publication of the novel. See the letters of January 6, 1925, April 11, 1925, and May 7, 1925, in *Letters of Thomas Mann, 1889–1955,* selected and translated by Richard and Clara Winston (New York, 1971).

[15.] Hans Castorp and Naphta are characters in *The Magic Mountain.* Kerényi argues elsewhere that the model for Naphta was the Hungarian Marxist critic Georg Lukács (b. 1885); see "Zauberberg-

As our correspondence began, Mann's own great entelechy had entered into a distinctive figure as never before, and after the completion of the third volume of the Biblical novel, into yet another, as if to supplement the first: That first was Joseph, a thoroughly Hermetic figure in Thomas Mann's characterization; and the other, the Goethe of the monologue that figures in a ghostly adventure of that aging gentleman.[16] He behaved like an aged Hermes with the aged Lotte, in spite of the fact that a mind nurtured on plaster-cast antiquity might see only the features of Zeus in him! I do not by any means wish to apply the Hermes theme everywhere, at any cost. Yet Thomas Mann's turning to mythology—that abandoned, at times apparently wholly forgotten passion of his childhood, the period of maternal care—actually took place through his identification with the Biblical youth, whereby the Biblical represented a *sanctioned* form of the mythological that may be extended deep into the sphere of ancient oriental religions, in accordance with the practice of Old Testament exegesis, and already neutralized in advance, in contrast to the forbidden, the *dangerous* form of myth.

"Mann's expert in matters of myth"—I could not have been that, at least at the start of our relationship, if only because the initial positions from which we approached mythology were too different. I had no use at all for "myth" as that incomprehensible force, at once comical and ominous, that developed in Germany between the two world wars and that Thomas Mann himself fully acknowledged: "myth" in the sense in which Ernst Bertram (to give a worthy example) understood it when he called his Nietzsche monograph—a book whose literary merits I readily appreciated—*Versuch*

---

figuren: Ein biographischer Versuch," in *Tessiner Schreibtisch* (Stuttgart, 1963), pp. 125–141.

[16.] The monologue of the aged Goethe is in chapter vii of *The Beloved Returns* (*Lotte in Weimar* [Stockholm, 1939]; *GW*, II).

einer Mythologie.[17] This represents perhaps a deficiency in me that may be connected with the lack of other elements that are usually present in Germans. I was a classical scholar devoted to Greek thought, nurtured in Hungary, when, in the winter of 1929 in Greece, I became sick of academic philology. I had nowhere encountered "myth" as a specific force, but "mythology" most definitely: dispersed through all the literature that had been handed down and in countless vase paintings that, far from being classified, had hardly even been surveyed at the time, not to mention the most impressive traces of all, those rare heads of divinities that have come to us from the hands of prehistoric sculptors.

Without being an archaeologist I had experienced the impact of direct contact with the material inheritance of antiquity. More and more I came to see my philological task in the written inheritance mentioned above—a task that could only be fulfilled by a method that had yet to be fashioned. A conviction grew in me then and has since remained unshaken: that by devoting myself wholeheartedly to this inheritance I could restore to its rightful place, namely, to a *central* place, an aspect of the life of antiquity that had been misunderstood

[17.] *Nietzsche: Versuch einer Mythologie* ("Nietzsche: An Exercise in Mythology"; Bonn, 1918). Ernst Bertram (1884–1957), professor of German literature, wrote this work during a period of close personal and intellectual contact with Mann during which Mann himself was at work on *Betrachtungen eines Unpolitischen* ("Reflections of a Nonpolitical Man" [Berlin, 1918]; *GW,* XII, 7–589). At the time Mann gave the Nietzsche book his wholehearted endorsement (see Mann's letter to Bertram of September 21, 1918, in *Thomas Mann an Ernst Bertram* [Pfullingen, 1960]). During the late twenties the friendship cooled as the political sentiments of the two moved increasingly far apart— Mann's toward a liberal cosmopolitanism and Bertram's toward a rigid nationalism culminating in adherence to the Nazi cause. A letter by Mann to Bertram on June 14, 1935, gives the reasons for the final break.

because of the errors of the Romantics and for other reasons—
I mean the religious aspect. If one reads those essays in which,
since the early thirties, I have sought to justify my position,
one will see how sparingly I have used the word "myth." I
carried this restraint to an extreme in my book about the religion of antiquity because of my distaste for a vague and confused modern concept. In the chapter in which I discussed the
phenomenon of mythology in its most comprehensible forms, as
transmission and inheritance, I wrote, "For this reason a discussion like the preceding one has avoided as far as possible
using this many-sided term ['myth']."[18]

In its Greek meaning, a myth—originally a true statement,
the sole factual account, later a mendacious statement—always
signifies the myth of *something*. The original meaning of "true
statement" was established by the perceptive Germanist André
Jolles;[19] the more exact sense of "factual account" was sup-
plied later by W. F. Otto.[20] The characteristically German
quality that I have never been able to accept is reflected in a
statement like this: "It is dynamic; it is endowed with a power;
it enters creatively into the process of life"—although the great
scholar and honored friend who could still print this in 1956
was referring to "veritable myth," the authentic and not the
false.[21] I was deeply saddened that the influence of myth in

[18.] *Die antike Religion* (Amsterdam, 1942), p. 17 (*The Religion
of the Greeks and Romans,* trans. C. Holme [New York and London,
1962], based on the 3d ed., rev. [Dusseldorf, 1952]).

[19.] See André Jolles, *Einfache Formen* (Tübingen, 1930, 1968), pp.
98 ff. The German term is "das wahre Wort."

[20.] See Walter F. Otto, "Gesetz, Urbild und Mythos," in *Die
Gestalt und das Sein* (Darmstadt, 1955), pp. 68 ff. The German term
is "der Sachverhalt."

[21.] The reference is undoubtedly to Walter F. Otto. The exact
quotation could not be traced, but similar formulations may be found
in numerous essays of the 1950's by Otto, particularly "Der Ursprüng-
liche Mythos im Lichte der Sympathie von Mensch und Welt," in

the false sense could thus make itself felt in Germany, or rather, that in Germany, and soon elsewhere too, people were ready to believe that a dynamic something called myth could exercise such an influence, irrespective of the direction it took. "The facts regarding the gods," concrete components of the tradition of antiquity, were of course already viewed by the early Christians as a corrupting force of the devil. For me they represented a combined product of man and his world, whether one considered the latter to be divine, as did the Greeks, or created by God, as did the Christians. It seemed to me that whoever opened men's eyes to the great teachings that emanate from the human-divine play of mythology also purified and humanized. Thomas Mann did this to a considerable extent by his brilliant analysis, in the lecture on Freud, of myth as an exemplary form of being in history.[22] As a Protestant and a German, however, he was rooted in the German situation, and this complicated his intellectual premises. His conscience was not altogether at ease—one may note this even in the first part of our correspondence—about his own mythological bent, which he connected with the maternal sphere of nature and which he considered only as a somewhat humanized form of the German conception of myth.

The actual, in no sense feigned, basis of our relationship was that he found me useful; and I, as a scholar, was gratified by the fact that the "great entelechy" was instinctively drawn to that innocent mythology—a spiritual activity allied to, and overlapping with, poetry, music, philosophy, and scholarship— that I had undertaken to establish. This may sound unkind, but it is both accurate and historical, and it in no sense ex-

---

Mythos und Welt (Stuttgart, 1962), and "Der Mythos und das Wort," in *Das Wort der Antike* (Stuttgart, 1962).

[22.] See "Freud and the Future," in *Essays of Three Decades* (New York, 1947), pp. 411–428 (*GW,* IX, 487–501).

cludes other feelings to which the letters testify: In our relationship, I was the observant, the warmer partner, he the creative, the colder. He husbanded his powers and resources with great self-awareness and discipline. In my writings he found, not only a store of unusual mythological materials, but evidently also some grounds for believing that works of mythology could be useful to mankind; and perhaps further, a source of confirmation in the midst of that intellectual excitement that took hold of him while reading, about which he has expressed himself so generously and which took him by surprise again and again like a secret passion. For he could always be astonished by himself. A great entelechy such as his could not be easily circumscribed; nor could the complications to which I have alluded be foreseen.

Thomas Mann was well aware of the wholly unpredictable activities of a great entelechy. His formulation of the issue is most pertinent, and incidentally corresponds to my own quite independent conception of mythology as a self-generation of the mythological material (mythology is to be differentiated from the development of an entelechy because of its dependence both on divine figures as its dramatis personae and on earlier—in fact, the earliest—never wholly extinguished examples of its own process). The formulation is to be found in the autobiographical account of 1930 in the *Neue Rundschau*: "But things—or whatever word better corresponds to the notion of the organic—have their own will, according to which they form themselves: *Buddenbrooks,* originally planned as the novel of a merchant in the manner of Kielland, at most 250 pages long, had had it; *The Magic Mountain* would insist on its own; and the story of Aschenbach too turned out obstinately to assert a meaning well beyond what I had intended to give it. The truth is that every work is a fragmentary yet meaningfully circumscribed realization of our essential nature; such realizations are the only, the difficult means for experiencing it at all, and it is no wonder that this cannot come about without some surprises." And later in the same text: "I felt from the start that the Davos story 'had something in it' that drew me along; it saw itself differently than I was able to in order to undertake it."[23] These are indications of a far-reaching identity between subject and object in the act of artistic creation. Later, in *The Holy Sinner* [1951], the active element is called "the spirit of storytelling." The term "great entelechy," on the other hand, stresses the continuity and coherence of all the "spirits of storytelling" that have been active in an artist's work. A "great entelechy" may well be affected by Christianity, may seek to throw it off, or may embrace it either occasionally or altogether; the unpredictability of such developments brought its surprises for Thomas Mann himself as well as for the observer.

In the fourth volume of the Joseph novel we find this profound statement of a humanistic harmony: "For the pattern and the traditional"—which apply to the true myth in its historical significance—"come from the depths which lie beneath and are what binds us, whereas the I is from God and is the spirit, which is free. But what constitutes civilized life is that the binding and traditional depth shall fulfil itself in the freedom of God which belongs to the I; there is no human civilization without the one and without the other."[24] Joseph speaks these words before the Sun King. I put them at the end of my *Töchter der Sonne* (1944),[25] to suggest the stability of a hu-

[23.] *A Sketch of My Life,* trans. H. T. Lowe-Porter (New York, 1960), pp. 44, 48 (*GW,* XI, 123, 126). Alexander Lange Kielland (1849–1906) was a Norwegian novelist. Gustav Aschenbach is the protagonist of *Death in Venice* (1913). "The Davos story" refers to *The Magic Mountain.*

[24.] *Joseph and His Brothers,* trans. H. T. Lowe-Porter (one-vol. ed.; New York, 1948), p. 937 (*GW,* V, 1422).

[25.] *Töchter der Sonne: Betrachtungen über griechische Gottheiten* ("Daughters of the Sun: Reflections on Greek Divinities"; Zurich).

manism that can also encompass the religion of the Bible. Yet what a strange impression the following words about *Doctor Faustus* made on me when he wrote again (September 23, 1945) after we resumed contact: "The pact with the devil is the main theme of the book, which covers the period from 1885 to the arrival of Hitler, but stands with one foot in the German sixteenth century. Will this be something for our classical philologian and mythologist? But a colleague of his writes it, and is infinitely devoted to the cold demon."[26] Remarkable words! The defense of humanistic harmony and human affection, qualities which could never be denied the narrator of the Joseph stories, is now left to a devoted observer. The "colleague" could only be Thomas Mann. But who may be perceived behind the "cold demon" to whom he was "infinitely devoted"? Was it Adrian Leverkühn,[27] as the context seems to indicate? Earlier he is called "veritably a son of hell"! Or the devil himself? Our *relationship*—humanist and philologian on the one hand, creative artist on the other—seemed clear enough, whatever might be mounted on it. But after all, was not the most incredible construct possible with Thomas Mann? And just as incredible a division and diffusion of his own personality?

I have already referred to the motto that I had chosen for the purpose. Now my task in saying what I wish to say is facilitated by Bengt Algot Sörensen's study in *Orbis Litterarum,* 1958: it spares me the need to analyze *Doctor Faustus* as an autobiographical document. I had read the novel—and been shaken, terribly shaken, and in an altogether different way than after reading any of his other works—before it reached me from his own hands. My letter about it, written from a certain distance, was sent almost at the same time

[26.] Kerényi omits the phrase "warm of heart" after "writes it," from Mann's letter of September 23, 1945.

[27.] The title figure in *Doctor Faustus*.

(September 11, 1948) that he dated the copy intended for me (September 12, 1948). I gave expression to my initial emotion by sending a small symbolic picture from my book *Der göttliche Arzt*.[28] It was from me that he had obtained the pain symbolism of "arrow-snake-shot-sting," which he represented by the engraved figure of a "winged snakelike monster" on the beryl facet of the precious ring given to Adrian Leverkühn. Now I sent him the picture of a coin with a similar monster: a winged snake, which, however, the healing god Asklepios carries on his back. I do not know whether he understood the symbol with which I meant to congratulate him on his recovery from what seemed to me the most anguished act of identification of his life.[29]

The embarrassing and tormenting question was, How could he make such a terrible simplification? Did not he himself call the claim that Nietzsche was somehow connected with the National Socialist barbarities the "grossest" of all confusions? And now he fashions a figure who, as he himself wrote me, "shares the fate of Nietzsche, of Hugo Wolf, etc., and is veritably a son of hell"—a figure endowed with the highest qualities of a great modern composer who enters into a pact with the devil—an act which is meant to express, through a Christian-mythological image, the guilt of the finest type of German intellect for National Socialism. This seemed unjust to me. Yet I was forced now to take into account the autobiographical elements that Sörensen had uncovered and scrupulously analyzed in his study, and I said to myself: "This is first of all—he himself! The great entelechy that had once entered into the blameless Joseph, now went into Adrian Leverkühn! And he is portrayed

[28.] *Der göttliche Arzt: Studien über Asklepios und seine Kultstätten* (Basel, 1947; Darmstadt, 1956; *Asklepios: Archetypal Image of the Physician's Existence,* trans. Ralph Manheim [New York and London, 1959]).

[29.] See Kerényi to Mann, November 17, 1947.

as a guilty criminal! A still greater injustice! Or else . . . "
A humiliating injustice to himself, a covert yet public confession (which is the term I dared use to him, since I did not know whether the stronger term "confession of guilt" corresponded to his own consciousness of his act)—this required an altogether different kind of judgment! Only a Christian would do this, a deeply committed Christian! I expressed this conviction when I saw him on June 14, 1949,[30] in Küsnacht, near Zurich: *"Doctor Faustus* is a Christian novel!" He wrote me later that this view "struck me and gave me a sense of satisfaction that comes with the truth." Nor did he forget that his reaction then had been to exclaim, *"You* should write about that!" [June 20, 1949]. I did not do so for the reason that I have already given in Wilhelm von Humboldt's words.

This, then, needs to be added to Sörensen's account. He cites the 1950 lecture "Meine Zeit," in which Thomas Mann spoke of his "guilt, indebtedness, obligation . . . as the object of religious anxiety, as something that urgently requires restitution, recovery, and justification."[31] Yet when the Danish scholar seeks the source of this astonishing self-identification in the "post-Romantic conception of the *Volk* as a corpus mysticum," he fails to do justice to the truly overwhelming fact that *Doctor Faustus* is a magnificent example of Christian self-censure and, for that very reason, also of the faith the great man kept with his nation. But who could ever do justice to this act hidden among so many other parts of the construct?

[30.] In the German edition Kerényi erroneously gives the date as June 14, 1948. See Kerényi to Mann, June 16, 1949.

[31.] Mann's statement is a more qualified one than the excerpt cited here. Mann's whole sentence reads, "If it is Christian to sense life, one's own life, in terms of guilt, indebtedness, obligation, as the object of religious anxiety, as something that urgently requires restitution, recovery, and justification—then those theologians who assert that I am the very type of the a-Christian writer are not altogether right" ("Meine Zeit" [1950], *GW,* XI, 302).

The humanistic harmony is restored by *The Holy Sinner,* the satyr play that followed the tragedy; one might almost have "ordained" this on objective grounds, on the basis of the inner form of the author's works. The great entelechy itself created the compensating act. But the pendulum did not yet come to rest: in accord with Hermetic law it needed to move back and forth between the two elements called "spirit" and "nature," bound to neither though participating in both. The old skirmish with Mother Nature, of which we find an early trace in the caricature from "Bilderbuch für artige Kinder" reproduced by Viktor Mann,[32] was taken up again. I received *The Black Swan* [1953] with the dedication "This small myth of Mother Nature." (*The Tables of the Law* [1944], after the Joseph novel, represents a similar swing of the pendulum.) And how does *The Confessions of Felix Krull, Confidence Man: The Early Years* end? With what a jubilant cry—of Mother Nature! What should have followed was a drama about Luther—the evocation of a balanced Christian reformer and a warrior of the devil, as was Savonarola in *Fiorenza.*[33] But the great entelechy sought and achieved something that then already seemed to me climactic, a stilling of the pendulum to which one might utter Faust's "Remain a while!" The eighty-year-old stood for the last time before an audience of friends and admirers during the celebration in his honor at the

[32.] "Picture Book for Good Children," a volume of parodies and drawings created jointly by Heinrich and Thomas Mann during their stay in Italy in 1897 and sent as a gift to their younger brother, Viktor, and to their two sisters, who were then living with the mother in Munich. See Viktor Mann, *Wir waren fünf* (Constance, 1964), for an account of this volume and a reproduction of a drawing by Thomas Mann of a smiling hag with a porcine face, dressed in a slip and corset, entitled "Mother Nature" (plate following p. 56).

[33.] Berlin, 1905 (*GW*, VIII); a drama based on the life of Girolamo Savonarola, the fifteenth-century Florentine reformer and martyr.

Zurich Schauspielhaus and read—"Krull in Defense of Love."[34] One thought of all the symptoms of "coldness" in his works and felt penetrated by a great, joyful sense of warmth.

Thus the period that had begun in 1945 came to an end. Not an easy period! Afterward there remained the overpowering sense of a spiritual vacuum: Thomas Mann signified so much. In our talks he had shown pre-eminently his gaiety and humor. These were related to his Hermetic nature, which favored irony, though not in a cutting, Apollonian fashion. Could it be that gaiety would be the last refuge of humanism in the face of those lifeless shadow forms that claimed to represent its substance? Yet the serious vein was never lacking in Thomas Mann: his occasional prose is full of a ripe and wise humanistic spirit, unsurpassed in its formulations.

After the war, the scholarly foundations of humanism needed to be established anew or (which is the same thing for a true scholarly discipline) needed to be set in motion again. Something of this sort occurs in the humanistic disciplines when they attain a level of objectification about themselves and are able to establish a direct relation to man and his field of experience. Nowhere could one sense a readiness for this. If one looked for more than a superficial humanism or if one expected the inner possibilities of such an intellectual orientation to be advanced by Thomas Mann or by one's own work, there was only disappointment. The task still remained, and it elevated and supported whoever recognized it. Humanism will probably always remain the source of such disappointment and such solace. Today I am glad to offer the documents of those years, documents which have had no worthy sequel. They bear witness to a painful destiny, but nevertheless a fortunate one.

[34.] From *Confessions of Felix Krull,* Book III, chapter x.

Ascona, September 8, 1944

The editor envisaged the publication of this correspondence in quite a different fashion—in later, quieter times, edited by a philologian from the circle of students mentioned in his first letter. The students are scattered now: in prison or in concentration camps, insofar as they are still alive, and restrained from any such task by evil, for so we must call this world-historical force—in Jacob Burckhardt's sense—although its present-day manifestations partake as much of common vulgarity as of evil. Those who return from its deadly compounds will have other work than concerning themselves with the private intellectual pursuits of an older generation, even if it is their own masters who are involved. And those who once perhaps considered themselves masters now wander in frightful isolation through a world of ruins, with no other companion than their own shadows, as did he who moved out early[35] from the house of the delusively triumphant "scholars." And they are fortunate still to possess at least their shadows—if, that is, they have not in their isolation also lost the roots from which something might still grow for the future.

In preparing this correspondence for publication, the editor looks for solace in his isolation. He seeks also to uncover for his own sake some of his roots, earlier stages of his development. But he does so in a manner proper to a philological, historical, *and* psychological investigator: in full view of those who would share the experience and the investigation. He is incapable of bearing without reservation the impersonality of the exclusively historical tradition of philology from which he himself derives. Behind every intellectual discipline there is hidden, after all, a more intimate *life* of the intellect—an *intellectual* life, of

[35.] Presumably Nietzsche. See note 36, below.

[25]

course, only insofar as all those deeper needs of the soul that are fulfilled in intellectual activity may be called intellectual in themselves. But this has decidedly not been the case in at least one branch of classical philology since about 1870. The difficulty is that if one wanted to speak of an underlying "intellectual life" governing the creative and pedagogic work of scholars in this area, one would also have to speak of an "intellect" inimical to free activity—which would be incongruous, a veritable *contradictio in adiecto.*

Ever since Ulrich von Wilamowitz-Moellendorff, that unambiguous spirit, won his scholarly victory over the divided German, the "self-prober, self-killer" Nietzsche,[36] we have lost the humanistic ideal of a *res publica doctorum virorum,* a free society of independent scholars, each working according to his own intellectual principles. In its place came a voluntary subordination to the despotism of a few narrowly specialized authorities wherever German universities, which meant chiefly Berlin, determined the pattern of classical studies and classical archaeology. One could speak at length here of psychological motivations in individuals, of the causes of the naïve self-assurance of a superficial scholarly tradition, but there is much less to say about any free life of the intellect. This is not to deny the value and necessity of all the preparatory work, the ordinary, daily trade of the philologian. But the great task of classical philology—the comprehension of antiquity—does not consist in such humble labor, whose skills are more easily learned than most outsiders, even prospective students, may believe.

[36.] Wilamowitz-Moellendorff (1848–1931), the leading classical scholar of his day, attacked Nietzsche's *The Birth of Tragedy* in an early pamphlet, *Zukunftsphilologie* (1872). From his position as professor in Berlin (from 1897) Wilamowitz exercised enormous influence not only within his own scholarly discipline but on German cultural life in general. Cf. Mann to Kerényi, July 15, 1936.

This is not the place to analyze the various *petits secrets des savants,* the deep-seated antipathies and sympathies, prejudices, and hopes that may even be found in an apparently sober discipline like philology, untouched, it would seem, by any existential or lyrical impulses. The chief task of the philologian must always remain—I wish to underscore it as a general principle here—interpretation, whether he confronts only the texts or an intellectual nexus that can never be wholly derived from the texts, a mythologem that may find its expression in monuments too. The better an interpreter is, the more he will also be an organ, both taking in and passing on: he is by nature one who, not only consciously but also unconsciously, reacts and acts. His whole being and existence, the structure of his mind, and his own experiences constitute an indispensable element of the interpretation, an element that cannot be eliminated but that must be revealed in fullest clarity. There should be no pretense of impersonality and no concealment of the personal where the personality of the researcher—who is, after all, a conscious observer and at the same time an unconsciously active organ—is so significant a factor in determining the results of the most scrupulous scholarly undertakings.

It is because this exchange of letters originated from an inner necessity of the participants, without any regard for future publication (the thought arose later, of course, but only after much had already been written), and because, in the treatment of intellectual matters, the editor's letters necessarily include highly personal matters, that he has deemed it proper not to withhold from publication any of his own letters or any personal data regarding himself. There is obviously no need to justify the fact that we publish here letters of Thomas Mann that provide the most reliable commentary possible on his mythological novel, an exceptional scholarly source for which there is hardly a parallel in world literature. But the publication of the letters at this time may be justified on two grounds:

[27]

first, the conclusion of the mythological novel about Joseph, followed by the Moses story *The Tables of the Law,* a work that is distinctly unmythological, in fact, postmythological in its conception, and that thus inaugurates a new stage of development for its author; and second, the evolution of the editor's mythological researches, which had their spontaneous beginnings in this correspondence. Let me explain this last point somewhat more fully.

In his last two letters [of Part I: February 18, 1941, and September 7, 1941] Thomas Mann welcomes the convergence of a scholarly study of mythology with psychology. He sees this as a means of reclaiming myth and "transmuting" it for humane ends in the face of irresponsible distorters who would misuse it for for political purposes. He himself, he says with reference to his *Joseph,* had long worked in this spirit. But he was able to bring about this "transmutation" consciously only because he had experienced in himself, in that fundamental human domain where it belongs, the spectacle of the primal and spontaneous functioning of the mythic material, the very life of mythology; and because he had presented this spectacle as an author and, yet more clearly, in self-reflection, as a writer of letters. He called this a "mysterious play of the mind"; and one would be justified in speaking also of "mysteries," both in the sense of antiquity, as the hidden experience of the mythic substance, and of Hölderlin,[37] as "more secret thoughts." But it was no Hölderlin, no German Romantic, not even a post-Romantic—it was someone standing in conscious contrast to Bachofen[38] who gave to the philologian and historian of re-

[37.] Friedrich Hölderlin (1770–1843), German Romantic poet who made extensive use of themes from Greek mythology.

[38.] Johann Jakob Bachofen (1815–1887), Swiss jurist and anthropologist whose major work, *Das Mutterrecht* (1861), argued for the existence of a matriarchal principle in early cultures. See Mann to Kerényi, December 3, 1945.

ligion this unique insight. Only thus was the humanistic scholar of religion liberated to become a mythologist, prepared to journey, together with Asclepiadean spirits, to the realm of the great mythologies. This represents the origins of "Die Geburt der Helena"[39] and "Was ist Mythologie?"[40] which led to the studies I prepared in collaboration with [Carl G.] Jung and to newer ones that have sought to recover the essence of archaic Greece, to *Hermes*[41] and *Töchter der Sonne*.

The present publication represents as well a sign of gratitude for that liberating impulse.

39. Given as a lecture in 1937 at the Doorner Arbeitsgemeinschaft of Wilhelm II, a group that was not under the influence of the Wilamowitz school. See Mann to Kerényi, December 6, 1938, note 2.

40. First published in *Europäische Revue,* 14 (1939), 3–18, and then as chapter i of the German and all subsequent editions of *Die antike Religion* ("What Is Mythology?" in *The Religion of the Greeks and Romans*).

[41.] *Hermes der Seelenführer: Das Mythologem vom männlichen Lebensursprung* ("Hermes the Guide of Souls: The Mythologem a Male Source of Life"; Albae Vigiliae, N.S. I [Zurich, 1944]).

PART I (1934–1945)

Mythology and the Growth of a Novel

Mann to Kerényi

My dear Sir,

I am most honored and pleased to have received your remarkable essay.[1] Let me express my sincere appreciation. You had a true sense of the fact that this study would be "something for me," that its subject lay close to my heart, and for this I am particularly thankful. I confess that the idea of a "dark," a "wolfish" Apollo was new to me, but I became accustomed to it immediately. The connections between mind and death (afterlife), between distance and knowledge (here we would have to take account of another concept dear to me, that of *irony*), and the insight that the spirit of Apollo may be perceived in that recuperative world, recuperative from *life*—all this touched the roots of my intellectual existence and delighted me.

My interest in matters of religious history and myth came only late, an inclination of maturer years that was not at all present in my youth. But now it is very active and will persist until the completion of that singular fictional project[2] of which the first volume, it seems, has come to your attention. I hope that the later parts (of which the middle one will appear in the spring) may also find favor with an expert like yourself, who has evidently dedicated his life to this vast and moving area of the human spirit.

My thanks again.

Sincerely yours,
Thomas Mann

[33]

1. "Unsterblichkeit und Apollonreligion," an offprint from *Die Antike*, 10 (1934); subsequently in all editions of *Apollon: Studien über antike Religion und Humanität* (Vienna, 1937; augmented ed., Düsseldorf, 1953). Translator's note: The German edition includes a facsimile of Kerényi's dedication on this offprint: "To the great author who gave us the figure of Herr Settembrini, and to one of the most profound historians of religion, K. Kerényi."
2. *Joseph and His Brothers.*

Kerényi to Mann

Budapest, February 7 (?), 1934

Honored Herr Doctor,

Your friendly lines gave me the greatest pleasure, and this not only because of the unexpected and undeserved honor, but also because of the almost unhoped for confirmation of what, in my lecture on Apollo, must have seemed the most daring scholarly speculation. For the scholar's way is, in this respect, particularly arduous. (You have correctly guessed that my life is dedicated to the history of religion and specifically, as a classical scholar, to that of antiquity. A book of mine on Greek-oriental fiction in the light of the history of religion [*Die griechisch-orientalische Romanliteratur in religionsgeschichtlicher Beleuchtung*] was published by J. C. B. Mohr, Tübingen, in 1927.) When the historical data indicate an overall structure (as in the case of Apollo) that cannot be comprehended in terms of the psychological clichés with which even some very eminent scholars seem to work, there remains only *one* proof of the deeper spiritual reality that may be assumed to underlie this general structure: this is the witness of great poets and authors, of explorers of the soul who stand in advance of their age in these matters. Your *Magic Mountain* has up to now

[34]

been such a witness for me with respect to the most delicate spiritual realities. But now *The Tales of Jacob* has become almost more precious and significant to me. There are insights there, such as the passages on "begetting and dying," "sex and death" (p. 285,[1] in a paragraph which is marvelous not only psychologically but also from the view of "classical scholarship"—I read it to a small circle of students with whom I was interpreting Plutarch's *De Iside et Osiride*), to which one may add "begetting and killing," that I myself have come to in the process of elucidating the nature of the satyrs as death divinities, but which I even now dare not lay before a "professional" public.[2]

Your inclusion of irony as an Apollonian concept is certainly correct, and first of all for Socrates himself. It was certainly no coincidence that that ironist Aldous Huxley gave the Apollo of Veii such a central role in his novella "After the Fireworks." He discerns the healing power of this divinity in his smile: "smiling at the sad, mysterious, beautiful absurdity of the world."[3] Besides yourself, it is primarily from English writers that I have learned to perceive "spiritual" realities in "mythological" forms—notably, from D. H. Lawrence and the great mythologist J. C. Powys. Is it too presumptuous to ask what your personal view of these two men is, if, that is, you have considered them? Both your Joseph novel and Powys' *A Glastonbury Romance* [1932] testify to the return of the European spirit to the highest, the mythic realities. In comparison, the field of scholarship often lags behind.

I take the liberty of sending you here two shorter papers, somewhat weighed down with undigested scholarly matter. One[4] is a kind of sequel to my Apollo essay; the other, a review, gives my conception of the bounds of Hades (pp. 364 ff.).[5] This notion is fundamental to my views on the history of religion (for example, with respect to Christianity); *The Magic Mountain* aided me much in establishing it. I am truly

[35]

grateful for untold enlightenment, stimulation, and, last but not least, enjoyment.

Sincerely yours,
Karl Kerényi

[1.] Refers to *Die Geschichten Jaakobs* (Berlin, 1933); in *Joseph and His Brothers,* pp. 191 f. (*GW*, IV, 293).

2. Today (1959), after twenty-five years, this would not be so exceptional; see Karl Meuli's afterword to Volume VII of Johann Jakob Bachofen's *Gesammelte Werke* (Basel, 1958), p. 500.

[3.] In *Brief Candles* (London, 1957), p. 242.

4. "Telesphoros: Zum Verständnis etruskischer, griechischer und keltisch-germanischer Dämonengestalten," *Egyetemes Philologiai Közlöny,* 57 (1933), 156 ff.

5. Review of Joseph Kroll, *Gott und Hölle* (Leipzig, 1932), in *Gnomon: Kritische Zeitschrift für die gesamte klassische Altertumswissenschaft,* 9 (1933), 363–371.

Mann to Kerényi

Küsnacht-Zch., February 20, 1934[1]

Dear Herr Professor,

Once more I found the greatest pleasure and stimulation in reading your fascinating letter and the two remarkable articles[2] you sent with it. Now that I have become familiar with these shorter samples of your work in religious history and mythology, I am resolved to study your major book on Greek and oriental fiction as soon as possible. I want to see how I take to it. Undoubtedly, there will be some embarrassment in realizing how limited my own command of this attractive and engrossing area remains. But the fact that *The Magic Mountain* and *The Tales of Jacob* can appear of lasting interest to a scholar like you supports my own inclination to proceed further. At the same time, your reaction confirms—or at least brings to mind again—the extent to which *The Magic Moun-*

tain (which has been considered exclusively in terms of its surface themes) touches on those interests and motives which, in the Joseph novel, become the explicit subject matter of the narrative. To put it another way: the degree to which the "sanitorium novel" serves as a connecting link between the realistic *Buddenbrooks* of my youth and the manifestly mythological work that emerged as I approached sixty.

Indeed, in my case the gradually expanding interest in myth and religious history is a "sign of old age." It corresponds to a taste that has, in the course of years, moved away from the bourgeois-individualistic toward the typical, the general, the universally human. In my youth it would have been out of the question to take pleasure in such a scene as the one you mention—Jacob's dream of Anubis—and in something like the answer of the jackal-headed boy: "I shall one day be rid of my head too."[3] This is almost a private joke, which most readers would pass over. But what is involved is the career of a god. For this Anubis, now still half beast and satyr-like, is the future Hermes-Psychopompos.[4] Have you noticed that I placed him on his rock exactly in the pose of the Hermes of Lysippos in Naples? I am very much in love with this statue, of which there is a fine copy in the Alte Museum in Berlin, and this passage is a secret expression of homage.

Of the English authors you mention I know two quite well. I admire in Huxley, notably in his essays, one of the most refined flowerings of the spirit of western Europe. I prefer him to D. H. Lawrence, who is undoubtedly a significant and characteristic phenomenon of his time, but whose hectic sensuality is little to my taste. I learned of Powys, not only from your letter, but also from an article in the *Neue Zürcher Zeitung* on his books *In Defense of Sensuality* [1930] and *The Meaning of Culture* [1929]. The article is entitled "Back to the Ichtyosaurus." Such a heading is, of course, not only rude but deliberately coarse in its approach, and yet its ridicule is not wholly without justification. There exists at present in European literature a kind of resentment at the development of man's cerebral nature, which has always seemed to me to be nothing but a snobbish and foolish form of self-abnegation. Yes, allow me to say that I am no friend of the movement directed against spirit and intellect, as represented in Germany, for example, by Klages.[5] I have long dreaded and combatted this tendency, perceiving its brutal and inhuman consequences before they had become manifest . . . That "return of the European spirit to the highest, the mythic realities" of which you speak so impressively is in truth a great and positive cultural movement, and I may claim that my own work has to some extent played a part in it. But I think that I may count on your support when I say that this *fashionable* "irrationalism" often involves a sacrifice, an adolescent throwing overboard of achievements and principles that constitute the essence, not only of a European, but of man himself. We are dealing here with a "back to nature" that is, in human terms, markedly less noble than that which laid the groundwork for the French Revolution . . . Enough! You understand me implicitly. I am a man of balance. I lean left by instinct when the canoe threatens to capsize to the right, and vice versa.

Allow me, after this digression, to speak once more of the indescribable delight I experienced in reading your study on the little Telesphoros with *cucullus*[6] and scroll. What an enchanting figure, this little death god! And particularly, what magic seems to be connected through the ages with the Capuchin's cowl! Strange! I had no suspicion of these things, and yet I gave my Joseph a cowl and a parchment roll after his resurrection from the well, as the Ishmaelites led him through Egypt. Such things reveal a mysterious play of the spirit and prove that a sympathy for scholarly lore can, to a certain extent, arise of itself.

With most respectful greetings, I am, dear Herr Professor,

Sincerely yours,
Thomas Mann

[1.] English versions of this letter and of Mann's letters of August 4, 1934, December 6, 1938, February 16, 1939, and December 3, 1945, were previously published in *Letters of Thomas Mann, 1889–1955,* selected and translated by Richard and Clara Winston (London: Martin Secker & Warburg, 1971; New York: Alfred A. Knopf, 1971); newly translated by permission.

2. See Kerényi to Mann, February 7, 1934, notes 4 and 5.

[3.] *Joseph and His Brothers,* p. 190 (*GW,* IV, 291). Anubis, in Egyptian mythology, was a god of the dead represented as a jackal. In Hellenistic times he was sometimes identified with the Greek god Hermes under the name Hermanubis.

[4.] Hermes as the guide of souls to the underworld. The role of Hermes in *Joseph and His Brothers,* and in Mann's work in general, has been extensively treated in the critical literature. For a review of the issue, with particular reference to this letter and to Mann's letter of March 24, 1934, see Manfred Dierks, *Studien zu Mythos und Psychologie bei Thomas Mann* (Bern and Munich, 1972), pp. 215–226.

[5.] Ludwig Klages (1872–1956), philosopher and psychologist, a leading exponent of the discipline of characterology.

6. Monk's cowl. Telesphoros, in Greek mythology, was a child god associated with Asklepios. See Kerényi to Mann, February 7, 1934, note 4.

Kerényi to Mann

Budapest, March 1, 1934

Dear Herr Doctor,

I never imagined when I first read *The Magic Mountain* ten years ago, and then twice again, that I might once hear the exceptionally appealing voice of Herr Settembrini addressing me personally. I have always felt how much you stood on *his* side. I am also familiar with your position on Bachofen in the *Pariser Rechenschaft.*[1] This has even been noticed in the philological journals (first by Professor Otto Weinreich of Tübingen in the *Philologische Wochenschrift,* 1930, 1120 f., and then by myself in *Gnomon,* 1934).[2] And now you have become a humanist in yet another sense. For the theory of religion is a humane and humanistic affair, certainly more so than humanistic "mythology" ever was. Yet in fact it has its source in this field, although its scope is much greater than that of the older humanistic studies of the gods. And today, again, it is primarily the classical divinities who are recognized as "higher realities" in a manner that is paradigmatic even for the study of unrelated, alien religions. (I had been accustomed to use this term for the mode of reality of the gods when a young friend pointed out to me that "higher reality" is already to be found in *The Magic Mountain*, where you speak of Hans Castorp's grandfather.) What you have to say about the history of religion is sometimes so astonishingly pertinent that it must come from mysterious depths, and this is now confirmed by the explanation that you have been kind enough to provide for certain details in the Anubis dream. That the jackal-headed boy sits on a stone corresponds precisely to the explicit meaning of Egyptian texts which name him simply as the one "on his rock." This was not your intention, of course (though you thus hit on an authentic element), since you meant to pay homage to a lovely Greek Hermes. I could not guess this from the sentence "I shall one day be rid of my head too." It was not that I passed over it, but I realized that I did not understand it. For as a historian of religion I may not confound the Greek god with the Egyptian.[3] Hermes in all his aspects is superbly depicted in Walter F. Otto's *Die Götter Griechenlands* (Bonn, 1929),[4] a book you absolutely must read, if you will allow me such a pressing recommendation. The jackal-headed boy is another matter. It is not he but, on a primitive level, a stone heap or a stone, the phallic herma,[5] which stands in the background of the classical Hermes figure. If, then, the stone points ahead to this figure, I am delighted that a parallel to the ancient Egyptian conception has been established through such a minute detail.

[40]

But then, those "backgrounds"! A great deal mixes and comes together there. W. F. Otto's descriptions of the classical gods are quite absurd if one hopes to grasp their essence simply in terms of their historical evolution; but they do reveal all kinds of gradations, such as the "wolfish" in Apollo, whose essential nature seems thus to coincide with that of barbarian wolf divinities: the same aspect of reality reveals itself in him as in them, although in Apollo it is in accord with the Greek spirit. One of the "backgrounds" of Hermes is that the phallic element is here related precisely to the realm of the dead, as a prominent archaeologist has claimed on the basis of hermae that were used as grave monuments.[6] For he is actually "a spirit of the night," "the genius of its virtue, its magic, its inventiveness, and its wisdom" (according to Otto), all that the "demonic night" signifies, "but with emphasis on its bolder, masculine side." The "background" proves that this "bolder side" is precisely the *phallic vigor,* irrepressible even in death, a force both destructive and fatal, still titanic and formless in the primal world, but also bestial and satyr-like, as you correctly depict Anubis. *His* essence is derived from the figure of an Egyptian nocturnal creature: he wears the head of a thief of corpses, since the nocturnal world manifests itself in him in Egyptian fashion. But if we leave that out of consideration, his essence is at least in part identical with that of Hermes (thus the later figure of Hermanubis). Therefore on this basis one may accept his statement that he will one day be rid of his head too. The same holds for what Aphrodite and Ishtar have in common. How lovely and true is Jacob's recognition of this fact when, pained for his own God, he kisses her image in her hour.[7] Of course, the Greek goddess in the context of her particular world is wholly distinct from the Babylonian, but she too participates in a background that extends far back, as her Greek epithet "the black one" reveals.

And this brings me back to D. H. Lawrence. I had long ago

worked out this darker side of Aphrodite and expounded it in my lectures, but never so concisely as I find it in his *Twilight in Italy:* "She is the gleaming darkness, she is the luminous night, she is goddess of destruction, her white cold fire consumes and does not create."[8] I am always impressed to see how Lawrence, as the great poet and sage he is, draws forth the positive from nature, which in itself is essentially mute, thus making it accessible to the spirit and a common heritage for humanity, whereas Klages, the theoretician, makes one feel primarily the negative aspect, in a heavy, oppressive manner. What this positive is I can perhaps explain in this way: one of the greatest and most human achievements of your *Tales of Jacob* is to have made us conscious of the horror that overcomes a man who has wasted his love on the "false one." I find this, in the best sense, in the spirit of Lawrence; similarly, the marvelous insight into moon worship at the beginning of the novel is close to Powys, just as in Powys himself, particularly in his *Wolf Solent* [1933] (also published by Paul Zsolnay), there is much of Thomas Mann. His theoretical books, which you mention, are also excellent and of a sublime intelligence.

But I do not want to burden you with these matters, particularly since I only now come to the most important point, which perhaps concerns not only me personally but scholarship in general. No one else can speak as authoritatively as you about the issues of the novel that I raise in my book. But the book is too much oriented to professional readers; it is in any case very much a work of my youth. I recently had to deal with the problem once more in a review for *Gnomon,* which has not yet appeared.[9] I am having a copy made of the central sections of this review and, with your permission, will send this to you along with my book in 8 to 10 days. Afterward, more on the following point: that the sequence *Buddenbrooks–Magic Mountain–Joseph* (as a *return* to the primal source of fictional narrative) is a kind of proof of my conception of the develop-

ment of the Greek novel (myth–fabulous tale–bourgeois narrative)—unless, that is, all this is an imposition on you.

With most respectful greetings,

Yours sincerely,

Karl Kerényi

[1.] In the autobiographical essay *Pariser Rechenschaft* ("An Ac-
counting from Paris"; Berlin, 1926), Mann makes a spirited attack on
Alfred Baeumler's attempt to rehabilitate Bachofen at the expense of
Nietzsche. See *GW*, XI, 48–51. Cf. Mann to Kerényi, December 3,
1945. On Mann's attitude toward Bachofen in general, see Dierks,
Studien, chapters ix and x.

[2.] In Kerényi's review of Ludwig Euing, *Die Sage von Tanaquil*
(Frankfort on the Main, 1933), in *Gnomon*, 10 (1934), 134.

[3.] See Mann to Kerényi, February 20, 1934, note 3.

[4.] English translation by Moses Hadas, *The Homeric Gods* (New
York, 1954).

[5.] A pillar with the significant mark of the male sex, usually sur-
mounted by the head of Hermes.

6. The reference is to Ludwig Curtius, whose position I was later
able to correct in my *Hermes der Seelenführer*.

[7.] See *Joseph and His Brothers*, p. 197 (*GW*, IV, 301).

[8.] D. H. Lawrence, *Twilight in Italy* (London, 1950), p. 60. Kerényi quotes in English.

9. Review of Rosa Söder, *Die apokryphen Apostelgeschichten und
die romanhafte Literatur der Antike* (Stuttgart, 1932), in *Gnomon*,
10 (1934), 301–309.

Kerényi to Mann

Budapest, March 13, 1934

Dear Herr Doctor,

I was very happy to receive your card from Arosa. The excerpt from the article is now ready, and I shall send the book
along with it too—nothing but fragments, as I now realize.[1]

But I have faith that you will perceive the essential core in all these fragments, since I have so often admired the sureness of your insight in this field. I was mistaken to publish my results still smelling of the workshop—trial efforts intended primarily for philologians. For it was precisely they who were least prepared for what was crucial . . . "Oui, ils sont charnel tous deux, l'amour et la mort, et voilà leur terreur et leur grande magie!"[2] It was too much to expect that they would recognize the role that death plays vis-à-vis love in the ancient Greek novel: one of affinity at the deepest level, which is, however, disclaimed on the surface. But the connection to the myth of Isis and Osiris is patently clear here. It represents, in fact, a general, human element, so there can be no question of borrowings but only of correspondences—though in any case the Greek novels are psychologically much shallower than *The Magic Mountain,* and the literary devices they utilize, as well as the religious and textual parallels amongst them, are perfectly obvious. Later too we see that the novelist walks the same narrow path, though less noticeably, between, on the one hand, the sphere of Egyptian mythology (notably the myths of death and eros) and all sorts of eruptions of a primitive world view, and, on the other, the domain of spirit (sometimes in a Christian or a materialist sense or crippled in some other way). Here too, in the fashion of antiquity, spirit manifests itself as *irony.* And it was this irony that made Petronius' subject matter—a world of picaresque companions oriented toward Priapus—into a novel.[3] It is the same with Huxley's *Those Barren Leaves* [1925] or *Antic Hay* [1923]. This represents the significance of Herr Settembrini vis-à-vis the "Hades" of *The Magic Mountain* . . . And now the new orientation: the *Glastonbury Romance,* with its magical, Celtic world in the background, and almost at the same time the exceptional achievement of *Joseph* . . . It appears that a confrontation with the mythical sphere becomes the crowning, the chosen task of the greatest novelists. The public views all this with some perplexity. I wonder whether one should not explain to the general reader, in simple, understandable language, that the novel at its acme now returns to its primal source and thus discloses its original essence. I have waited seven years so far to undertake a thorough revision of my theme of 1927, and I could perhaps wait still longer (I am now 37 years old) for a more propitious time.[4] I would be most grateful to learn your opinion and suggestions. Your views are crucial for me in determining whether the essential form of the novel as I saw it in my studies of the comparable genre of antiquity is not merely an artificial and arbitrary construct.

With most respectful greetings,

Yours sincerely,
Karl Kerényi

[1.] About the article see Kerényi to Mann, March 1, 1934, note 9. The book is *Die griechisch-orientalische Romanliteratur in religionsgeschichtlicher Beleuchtung*.

2. "Yes, both of them, love and death, are of the flesh and therein lies their terror and their potent magic!" (*The Magic Mountain* [New York, 1961], p. 342 [GW, III, 476]).

[3.] Petronius Arbiter (1st century A.D.) was the author of the Roman picaresque novel *Satyricon*. Priapus was a fertility god whose symbol was the phallus.

4. I have since taken up this subject only in a lecture. See Mann to Kerényi, September 9, 1938, note 1.

Mann to Kerényi

Küsnacht-Zch., March 24, 1934

Dear Herr Professor,

The end of our stay in Arosa and a further trip to Basel have regrettably delayed my thanks for the interesting letter of the

13th and the most valuable gift of your book.[1] Forgive me, and please accept, though in much briefer form than I am tempted to undertake, this expression of my sincere gratitude and of my susceptibility to your exceptional intellectual gifts! Your book, which I have already gone through, is for me a source of the most pleasurable, if often only vague and general, stimulation. I admire its astonishing erudition; I love its flair for analogies, which is transmitted to the reader and makes him productive, so that he suddenly sees relationships in world literature which would never have occurred to him otherwise. What, for example, was the relation of *Cervantes* to the Greek novel? Did he know and use it? By coincidence I am just reading *Don Quixote* again, or rather, am reading it for the first time thoroughly and to the end. There are episodes in it that show a striking correspondence with motives from Heliodorus and *The Golden Ass*.[2] The story of the mock dagger, for example (p. 31 of your book), has an exact parallel in one of the novellas of *Don Quixote*, where a country wedding is broken up by the seemingly tragic suicide of the rejected lover, and the bloody deed then reveals itself, to the total surprise of the reader, as a grotesque game. Still more striking is the story of the braying asses in *D.Q.*: the two aldermen, both excellent brayers, who vied in imitating an ass, and the *beating* of one of them precisely because of his braying. Do you know any explanation for these similarities? Maybe it is this: the Greek novel has strong ties with the Orient. But the Italian novella— Boccaccio, for example,—was also indebted to the Orient, drew motives from it. Boccaccio could have been the bridge between Cervantes and the Greek novel. Excuse this dilettantish conjecture!

Altogether, there is something marvelously enticing and mysterious in the world of "correspondences" [*Beziehungen*]. The word itself has for a long time enchanted me, and what it signifies plays a pre-eminent role in all my thinking and artistic

[46]

activity. Since reading your book, I have no doubt that a relationship born of inner necessity and intuition will reveal itself between my Joseph epic, particularly its third, Egyptian
volume, and the Greek novel of late antiquity with its oriental
influences; all this affects me in a supernatural, humorous
manner. I only need to read a sentence like that in your note
on p. 254—"To play a god, for the primitive mind, always
signifies to a small extent to be the god"—in order to become
aware of this relationship of ideas, this instinctive affinity. It is
certainly true that my Joseph furthers his own career by means
of a dazzlingly crafty adaptation of the Tammuz-Osiris pattern, which allows him, along with the beauty of his "appearance," to induce men to take him partly, yet rather more than
less, for a god, for *the* god. The idea that this deception has a
higher justification because of a fundamentally *real* mythical
identity is something I have "taken" from the novel of antiquity—without knowing it. And in my third volume, how significant will be the theme of *"virginity* in distress triumphantly
sustained"!³ You can imagine with what attention I read your
discussions of this remarkable theme.

The typewritten material you sent me was an important and
welcome supplement to your book. I need hardly add that I
welcome your plan to write on the reversion to myth in the
modern novel, a reversion to be understood as a veritable
*home*coming. I urge you to carry through this exceptionally
interesting idea. One of the noblest tasks of philological criticism is to elucidate and reveal the significance of movements
of this kind in the more naïve and spontaneous regions of the
life of the mind. The concurrence of cases proves that your researches have to do, not with any artificial construct, but with
a living reality. I can by chance offer you a further example:
Alfred *Döblin,* whose inclination toward the mythical has for a
long time wavered between the latent and the manifest, is now
at work on a Marduk novel, something like the wanderings of

[47]

the Babylonian god.[4] Very strange! Perhaps you can wait for the appearance of this work, perhaps also for the third volume of my *Joseph*. But of course, it is possible even now to speak definitively about this matter from your point of view.

I have just received copies of *Young Joseph* and will have one sent to you to accompany these lines.

I had planned a more detailed letter, though this one has been delayed long enough. I would have liked to return to some of the points that you raised in an earlier letter, such as the question of Bachofen, the history of religion as a humanistic pursuit, or Hermes, my favorite divinity. Another time! Much correspondence has piled up, and I must close. I now have Otto's book and shall begin reading it as soon as I have finished yours.

With warm greetings,

Yours sincerely,
Thomas Mann

[1.] *Die griechisch-orientalische Romanliteratur.*

2. In my *Die griechisch-orientalische Romanliteratur in religionsgeschichtlicher Beleuchtung,* I deal with Heliodorus' *Aethiopica* and the various versions of *The Golden Ass* (in Lucian and Apuleius); and also with the theme of beating and its religious background. Thomas Mann took this up again in detail in the volume *Leiden und Grösse der Meister* (Berlin, 1935). See "Voyage with *Don Quixote,*" in *Essays of Three Decades* (New York, 1947) (*GW*, IX, 427–477).

[3.] See *Die griechisch-orientalische Romanliteratur,* p. 210.

[4.] *Babylonische Wandrung oder Hochmut kommt vor dem Fall* (Amsterdam, 1934).

Kerényi to Mann

Budapest, April 7, 1934

Dear Herr Doctor,

Returning from Italy after a short vacation, I find your long, enchanting letter, as well as your book [*Young Joseph*], which would have been a "gift" for me even if you had not sent it as a gift, more valued still on account of your dedication. Thus it is veritably *duplex dos libelli*.[1] And the book itself is no mere *libellus* but something truly great, which probes to the very depths of man's nature and of more still. I say this on the basis of what I already know from it (from *Die Neue Rundschau*): Joseph's talk with the "guide."[2] I found occasion to cite the god's words about human beauty in connection with a newly discovered fragment of a mime by Sophron, which I succeeded in interpreting just before my departure. I will write no more about it now, since my essay is to appear in an Italian periodical.[3] I also want to come back to your interesting observations about Cervantes in my lext letter. I am eager to know what you will write me regarding Bachofen, the history of religion as a humanistic pursuit, and Hermes (perhaps also Otto). For the moment, I only hasten to send you my most recent study, "Satire und Satura," as a modest sign of my gratitude.[4] I am almost ashamed to impose on you with this, for I would find it most valuable to know your views about the Dionysian, as well as about the nature of satyrs and satire . . . Please accept my apologies and thanks.

Yours sincerely,
Karl Kerényi

1. "The little book twice a gift."
[2.] See *Joseph and His Brothers,* p. 363 (*GW,* IV, 541 f.). This

passage is part of an excerpt first published in *Die Neue Rundschau,* 43, Part II (1932), 205–226.

[3.] See Kerényi to Mann, December 31, 1934, note 1. Kerényi views the guide as a manifestation of Hermes (see *Apollon,* pp. 154 f.).

4. "Satire und Satura," *Studi e materiali di storia delle religioni,* 9 (1933), 129–156.

Mann to Kerényi

Zurich-Küsnacht, April 24, 1934[1]
Schiedhaldenstrasse 33

Dear Herr Professor,

I cannot any longer delay thanking you for your letter of the seventh of this month and for the literary gift that accompanied it,[2] however brief and meager my message must be at this time. Along with my current work, I am very much taken up these days with various travel and lecture engagements in this country, and at the same time somewhat preoccupied by the prospect of a trip to America in the near future, where my presence is desired in connection with the appearance of the Anglo-American edition of *The Tales of Jacob.* The decision was made suddenly, and the plans still need to be worked out. As it now stands, I do not even have a proper visa for the trip and am dependent, as in the cases of France and of Switzerland, on the good graces of the American authorities.

Thus it is impossible for me at the moment to enter into the questions that have occupied us in our correspondence. But I do want to send you my warm thanks for the excellent hours that I have spent with your new work. Its erudition, infused with so much thought and wit, has made them most enjoyable hours; and it is seldom that a profound knowledge of the past is so happily combined with the contemporary creative spirit.

No more for today, then. I hope still to find a few quiet hours before my departure to chat with you in writing about matters that interest both of us.

With friendly greetings and good wishes,

Yours sincerely,

Thomas Mann

1. Typewritten.
2. See Kerényi to Mann, April 7, 1934, note 4.

Kerényi to Mann

Budapest, April 30, 1934

Dear Herr Doctor,

When I received your friendly letter I had already finished reading *Young Joseph,* though I was by no means done with the book, just as one is never "done" with [Goethe's] *Faust II.* This is undoubtedly to be attributed to the Hermetic nature of this work. There was already something Hermetic in Hans Castorp's "journey of maturation," insofar as he was dependent on a guide within "Hades" and out of "Hades." It is no accident that I think of *Faust II* in this connection: the way to the "Mothers," to the "Classical Walpurgis Night," to the sphere of the Lemurs, to wherever the heathen and the Germanic come together—all these are Hermetic ways, in that primary mythic sense that has not been achieved elsewhere in post-heathen Europe. ("Of the gods they honored chiefly *Mercury* . . . "—Tacitus, *Germania,* chapter 9.) We now possess, in addition to the Hermetic "myths" of the Germanic tradition, your Hermetic "novel," in *precisely* the sense that I believe I placed the novel alongside the form of myth. I find even in *Young Joseph* a very clear statement to justify this notion of the nature of the novel: "Who will say . . . where the stories are originally at home, whether above or below?" (on page 65).[1]

It is this very *question* that indicates the Hermetic point at which this novel is situated (corresponding to that of Faust in the "Dark Gallery": "Then sink! I could as well say, 'Rise!'"[2] It represents a Biblical ἑρμηνεία[3] in both the purely mythical and the simply human sense. I often felt a kind of dizziness in being led between these two realms, as if in a dream, yet with a lucid, in fact an exceptionally alert, mind that was bound to know along what a precipitous edge you were taking me. Charm of the divine, charm of the all too human, and charm of the spirit that "opens" the way in both directions: this is a true ἑρμαῖον,[4] a Hermetic accomplishment in itself, but also for you, who never before anticipated an achievement in the field of religious history; and at the same time a Hermetic find for the rest of us, for whom a confrontation with Hermes himself in a great and wholly modern work of art comes wholly unexpectedly. As a historian of religion I could not help but admire your mastery of the difficult and perilous subject matter (Israelite, Phoenecian, Babylonian, etc.); but your dedication to the Hermetic spirit (even in details, like the characterization of Naphtali, p. 127)[5] is something that I must view as a *datum* of religious history and that I have ventured to place beside the Homeric "Hymn to Hermes" and Sophocles' "Hunters"[6] as primary evidence. I refer not merely to the cited passages, but to the whole novel. For me this is the key to its ambiguity, its unimaginable abundance. I stand rapt and mute before this abundance and say to myself, so as not to remain inarticulate, only what any ordinary reader ignorant of mythology might say: "I liked this volume even more than the first. What a shame that one must still wait for the third."

This unpleasant necessity of having to wait is not easy to bear. And when I recall what you wrote about the next volume in that long, exceptionally interesting scholarly letter! [March 24, 1934]. The novel of Joseph is already closely related to the Greek novel by its Hermetic standpoint between myth and purely human history. When we add the "love story," as well as Joseph's—not only the poet's—playful contact with the divine, then the reversion to the stage at which Cervantes found the novel of antiquity will have been accomplished. For I am convinced that he read both *The Golden Ass,* of which there already existed in the sixteenth century a fine edition by the humanist [Filippo] Beroaldi, and Heliodorus. The latter was already translated into Latin at the time. Your demonstrations of correspondences are cogent and do not require even the assumption of any intermediaries to explain them.

I also want to thank you specifically for the most recent, shorter letter. Your opinion regarding my work and its relations to the contemporary creative spirit means more to me than that of all the learned academies. That you also found evidence of this spirit in my "Satire und Satura" is most heartening and gives me renewed strength to continue on that difficult path that I undertook with my study of the Greek novel and then continued with my essay on Apollo and this last one on the "Dionysian" and the "satyr-ic." I hope that you will have time, at least on your return from America, to come back to these questions and that you will not forget me altogether during your stay there. Of course, one cannot expect too much from America with respect to a dedication to "higher realities" (how lovely to find this phrase now in *Young Joseph* in a religious-historical context!). Yet even there one can hope for a humane spirit that knows how to value, both in art and scholarship, a fusion of the most ancient and the newest when it occurs in a peaceful, *Hermetic manner* (he is, after all, φιλανθρωπότατος θεός).[7]

So I wish you the protection of Hermes for the trip to America and your activity there.

My most respectful greetings.

Yours sincerely,
Karl Kerényi

[1.] Refers to the Berlin, 1934, edition; in *Joseph and His Brothers,* p. 292 (*GW,* IV, 439).

[2.] Goethe, *Faust,* l. 6275 (Part II, Act I).

3. Exegesis.

4. "Fortunate find"—understood as a gift of Hermes.

[5.] Refers to the Berlin, 1934, edition; in *Joseph and His Brothers,* pp. 327 f. (*GW,* IV, 490).

[6.] Or "Ichneutae," a satyr play of which fragments have survived. It deals with the theft by Hermes, soon after his birth, of Apollo's cattle.

7. "The most friendly of gods to man."

Mann to Kerényi

Küsnacht-Zurich, August 4, 1934
Schiedhaldenstrasse 33

Dear Herr Professor,

I deeply regret not having thanked you yet for your most recent piece of criticism[1] and hope that I can make up for it, late as it is. I have been a poor correspondent in recent days, not only for you but for everyone. You know what the chief cause has been: our trip to America, which has cost me at least a month in any case and has created no little confusion in the whole of my modest economy. Altogether, it was really a first-class lark, by which I mean to suggest both the impressive and the useless side of the affair. I do not want to regret the adventure, for it certainly had its appealing and personally justifiable side—this gathering in of sympathy that has been sown and nurtured over the years, especially when the harvest at home has been leveled by hail.

The difficulty was that soon after my return, when I had just begun my habitual schedule again, yet another trip intervened: this time to Venice, to what was in fact a rather tiresome international congress on the arts. The only gain was to see once again what has long been, and for deep-seated and complex reasons, that dearly beloved city together with its resort islands, the locale of a certain tale now already twenty years old.[2] For half of that period I had not been there, but this chance visit has broken the ice; and, if we live and the situation of Europe permits, I hope to spend a couple of weeks there next spring without indulging in fruitless twaddle about such subjects as "L'art et l'état" or "L'art et la réalité."

Having brought up this problematic "situation"—and who knows how much more problematic yet in the future?—I have come to the issue that troubles me most, one that has affected my rest, my serenity, my need for concentration, my spiritual and even physical well-being, in short, my productivity. I do not know how you as a scholar stand with regard to the events of the day, to politics or what is called world history, but I suspect that you are able to remain inwardly more detached from all this than I—much to my shame, I would add, did I not have the excuse that these events are chiefly centered in my homeland, from which I am banished,[3] and that therefore my relation to them is necessarily much more immediate and, to use Goethe's term, "pathological" than yours. Throughout this past year and a half I have sought to counteract the unremitting grief brought on by the fate of my country—that fate that threatens to make over the whole continent in its image—by carrying on and completing my personal tasks in an upright spirit, though with varying success. But I cannot express how much I have been overcome by the atrocities of June 30, the horrors in Austria, and then the coup d'état of that individual, his further elevation, which undoubtedly signifies a new stabilization of his hitherto shaky regime.[4] How terribly all this has upset me, alienating me from those matters which, if my heart were firmer and colder, would certainly be my sole, most immediate concern! What do I care about "world history," I should perhaps think, as long as they allow me to live and work? But I cannot think thus. My moral and critical conscience is in a continual state of irritation, and I am increasingly incapable of indulging in the, it may well be, sublime play of my fictional work without yielding to the need to speak my piece, to unburden my heart of all the perturbation, knowledge, painful experience, and also hatred and contempt that lie in it.

Thus, in all likelihood, I shall pass from narrative fiction to some direct, personal form, as in the time of the *Betrachtungen eines Unpolitischen*,[5] and the completion of my third volume will be put off to a more distant future. So be it. A man and writer can only do what he feels compelled to. The fact that the world crisis is also a crisis in my life and work is in the order of things and should serve me as a sign of my vitality. The time seems to me ripe for a statement such as I have in mind, and the moment could soon come when I would regret having extended my waiting silence beyond its proper period.

I wanted to tell you all this to bring you up to date. Once more my thanks for your essay. What new and unexpected interrelations again! You may rest assured that in my own meditations I shall hold fast to the world of interests we share.

Sincerely yours,
Thomas Mann

1. Review of Ludwig Euing, *Die Sage von Tanaquil* (Frankfort on the Main, 1933), in *Gnomon,* 10 (1934), 134–139.

2. *Death in Venice.*

[3.] Mann was on a lecture tour abroad when the burning of the Reichstag on February 27, 1933, unleashed the first wave of official persecution against opponents of the Nazi regime. Although his house in Munich was soon confiscated, his daughter Erika managed to bring out his manuscripts, including the Joseph novel. Mann was not to return to Germany until 1949.

[4.] On June 30, 1934, in the notorious blood purge, Hitler had numerous leaders of his own party, as well as other opponents, summarily executed. An attempted Nazi coup in Austria on July 25 resulted in the assassination of the Austrian chancellor, Engelbert Dollfuss. On August 2 the German president, Paul von Hindenburg, died, whereupon Hitler assumed the office of president together with that of chancellor.

[5.] Originally published in 1918; see Introduction, note 17.

Kerényi to Mann

Lumbarda, Korcula Island, August 13, 1934

Honored Herr Doctor,

Your long awaited letter reached me yesterday on this lovely Dalmatian island where the arrival of the mail is in any case a special occasion, since it comes only four times a week. Your letter made it all the more important for me. The envelope had to be cut with the thorn of an agave—and I found in my hands another sad confirmation of what has also been for me the outsider (neither German nor Jew) a torturing experience during these recent days. I have been on this island for two weeks now and read no papers, since I do not understand Croatian, which is spoken here. All I know of the most recent events is that Hindenburg has died.[1] But at the end of June, when I gave a lecture in Frankfort/M.[2] (in honor of the sixtieth birthday of Walter F. Otto, whose book you will have read by now), I visited, both there and during my trip, many old friends and colleagues. What I want to write you, however, is not based on their direct statements or, in fact, on any form of "communication." Let me be quite explicit about this. *This*

—not being able to express oneself and only the boldest, the most worthy and respected daring to do so on occasion—is of course also part of the "situation." And you will understand me when I ask you to consider this expression of mine as absolutely confidential. For it could be found out with whom I was in contact in Germany (in Frankfort I was the guest of a world-famous scholar), which could lead to frightful consequences for those individuals.

What I experienced can be put very briefly: I had the impression of unspeakable suffering in those of spiritual substance, of mute concurrence and cooperation by the average citizen, and of greedy, driving ambition in all of the worser sort. And I must confess that I would worry very little about the average man were it not that the weight of the masses is concentrated in him, a weight which threatens to crush the world of intellect and its representatives. The German "intelligentsia" *has* already collapsed. But what will be frightful will be the collapse of a higher, spiritual sphere: the fate of Hölderlin and Nietzsche monstrously multiplied, and the triumph of precisely that force against which only Hölderlin and Nietzsche represent a possible counterforce for men of intellect everywhere, not only in the German situation.[3] Or will the world of the average man be finally shattered through the world of intellect, even if the intellect remains *mute?* I believe in Apollo and his effortless victory. In the meantime, however: *Qui tacet, consentire videtur.*[4] And in all this I do not think that I have spoken one word from a "political" perspective.

Nor do I in adding something that is perhaps still more terrifying: the nasty, un-Dionysian (dys-Dionysian, I might say) insanity of the youth. (I have just read in an author of the George-Kreis[5] of the "Nordic god who bears in himself the will to self-destruction and hastens toward the twilight of the gods.") The youth in Germany today are being reared in the atmosphere of this insanity, and, insofar as it is still possible, they (and the world) must be saved from it. I have watched this youth—a *whole* city—march out one Saturday evening in Heidelberg, in long columns, under flags and in uniforms marked by symbols of death; I was forced to listen to their battle songs and combat games the whole night through; this was perhaps the most sorrowful moment of my life, just because I am passionately devoted to a heroic youth. I stayed for ten days in Austria, shortly before the recent bloody events, and in fact just at their center, near Leoben. I was disgusted there by something like a rotten smell and could not stay. The same insanity flared up then in those very events. And I must ask whether you in Switzerland, especially if, with your respected and potent voice, you now express yourself as you wrote me you intended to, are really safe? Please forgive my concern, but this insanity respects no boundaries.

In the meantime my circumstances have been altered in the sense that I have now been given a chair of my own at the University of Pécs (Fünfkirchen) and am obliged to spend part of the year there. I shall remain in Lumbarda until August 25 and then in Budapest until September 15.

My devoted greetings.

Sincerely yours,
Karl Kerényi

[1.] See Mann to Kerényi, August 4, 1934, note 4.

2. *Dionysos und das Tragische in der Antigone,* Frankfurter Studien zur Religion und Kultur der Antike, XIII (Frankfort on the Main, 1935).

[3.] Both men were afflicted by insanity during the last years of their lives—Friedrich Hölderlin (1770–1843), the poet, from 1806; Friedrich Nietzsche (1844–1900), the philosopher, from 1889.

4. "Whoever keeps silent seems to acquiesce."

[5.] The "George circle" was a literary school of a neo-Romantic, elitist orientation, led by the German poet Stefan George (1868–1933). The quotation could not be identified.

Kerényi to Mann

Budapest, December 31, 1934
II. Kapy-u. 10

Honored Herr Doctor,

On the last day of this sorrowful, oppressive year let me pay my respects to you with good wishes for the new year. I am sending at the same time the German text of my piece about Sophron and Greek naturalism. It will appear shortly in an Italian translation in the *Rivista di filologia classica*.[1] I should like to ask you to glance also at the first issue of a Hungarian periodical that has been founded by very young people, mostly students of mine, for the purpose—as they say—of furthering the spirit of humanism, serving the discipline of classical antiquity, investigating humanism in Hungary, and laying the basis for a humane central Europe in which to follow the path of humanistic scholarship. The whole idea originated with the young people; they took only their guardian god from my lecture on Apollo. Would you allow me to give them your letter concerning this god, so that they may publish it in their *Apollo?* I enclose a copy of that first letter you sent me, such a precious one to me, and ask that you decide about the publication only according to your feeling.

With devoted greetings,

Sincerely yours,
Karl Kerényi

1. "Sophron oder der griechische Naturalismus," in Italian in *Rivista di filologia e d'istruzione classica*, 63 (1935), 1–19; German version in *Apollon.*

Mann to Kerényi

Küsnacht-Zurich, January 6, 1935
Schiedhaldenstrasse 33

My dear Herr Professor,

Sincere thanks for your remembrances on the new year. Let me warmly reciprocate your good wishes! I have not yet been able to read what you so kindly sent me. There was a great bustle of children and guests in our house during the holidays; I have been somewhat worn out by it. Quiet and a regular tempo are, after all, the best that people like us can wish for, and yet one can't take it for the duration. But how much I hope that this state of exhaustion in which I now find myself will soon pass, for in about two weeks I am to undertake a journey that will also bring me to Budapest on January 27. I am to hold a lecture there about Richard Wagner that morning, in the Belvárosi Szinház, and this will give me the occasion, I trust, to shake your hand in person for once and to thank you for much stimulation, as well as for your warm interest in my existence.

Let this news of my plans suffice for today! I enclose my earlier letter. I am happy to offer it to *Apollo*.[1]

Yours sincerely,
Thomas Mann

1. The letter of January 27, 1934, was first published in that Hungarian periodical.

Kerényi to Mann

Dear Herr Doctor,

I have been home again since the beginning of May, and in this period, until two days ago, I have actually read only in your new book on the "masters."[1] In earlier days it was different. For example, I devoured *The Magic Mountain* when I was first given the Hungarian translation. I had not intended to read it in Hungarian but only to glance at it, but I read it straight through in Hungarian and then again in German. It went differently with the *Joseph*. I felt compelled repeatedly to pause so as somehow to hold on to the pleasure that the individual pages gave me.

Now with the [*Leiden und Grösse der*] *Meister* it was again somewhat different. My interest impelled me to read quickly, as with *The Magic Mountain*. But I was restrained, not only by my pleasure in its "plasticity," but also by my admiration of its "criticism," in the sense in which you contrast this notion with formal "plasticity" in your second essay on Goethe. It was this essay and the one about Storm—with whom I had actually felt little contact—that moved me most;[2] I was struck in both essays by your precise, scholarly formulations of such difficult and elusive realities, such as—to call one by its name, now that you have shown the way—by the "quality of immortality."

I have long been occupied with this quality in Greek literature in particular, and it was this that I wished to suggest in my Florence lecture[3] when I spoke there of a "claim to permanence" that spiritual products possess independently of the written text; but of course I had not come upon your "formulation" . . . I am sending you this lecture now as it was given at the Congress for Papyrology; it will only appear in print in the fall.

I followed your sea voyage with *Don Quixote*[4] with exceptional interest, for reasons that you will guess. The honor you paid me by mentioning my book, and the way in which you mentioned it, is truly the greatest that has come to me so far. I thank you for that and also for the dedication. Incidentally, I was reminded of a sea voyage to Kos and Rhodes, which I always connected also to the atmosphere of your *Joseph* . . .

And since I speak of recollections, let me say how gladly I recall your visit to Budapest. I was particularly struck by the youthfulness and vitality of your nature. Indeed, in looking back, I realize that you belong to the classic writers of my own youth. And now how astonishing to think that we may congratulate you these days on your sixtieth birthday [June 6, 1935].

Allow me to do so again from the bottom of my heart.

With devoted greetings,

Sincerely yours,
Karl Kerényi

1. *Leiden und Grösse der Meister.*
[2.] "Goethes Laufbahn als Schriftsteller" ("Goethe's Career as a Man of Letters"), *GW*, IX, 333–362; "Theodor Storm" (1817–1888, German poet and fiction writer), *GW*, IX, 246–267); both in *Essays of Three Decades,* pp. 46–65, 270–286.
3. "Die Papyri und das Wesen der alexandrinischen Kultur," in *Atti del IV. Congresso Internazionale di Papirologia* (Milan, 1936); and in *Apollon.*
[4.] "Voyage with Don Quixote." See Mann to Kerényi, March 24, 1934, note 2.

Mann to Kerényi

[Under a printed text expressing thanks for congratulations on his sixtieth birthday; mailed from New York, June 19, 1935.]

With warmest greetings and thanks from the middle of the ocean. I shall write as soon as I can. The confusion was great and I have much work to clear up.

Thomas Mann

Mann to Kerényi

Küsnacht, September 6, 1935

Dear Herr Professor,

My heart-felt thanks for the lovely essay,[1] which I read with true enjoyment. It is perfectly remarkable what a stimulating effect your pieces always have on me. Even as I was reading this, I suddenly felt an impulse again to continue spinning my own thread. You will soon receive an expression of appreciation for the kind words[2] you contributed to Bermann's box.[3] Forgive the use I made of a facsimile! This kind of circular letter is in any case a little more direct than a printed one. We have just returned from Salzburg, where we saw lovely things and where I also read a new chapter from the Egyptian part of the *Joseph* [*Joseph in Egypt*].

Sincerely yours,
Thomas Mann

[1.] See Kerényi to Mann, June 4, 1935, note 3.

[2.] Kerényi's message, reproduced in facsimile in the German edition, reads as follows:

Honored Herr Doctor,

Doctor Hermeticus, I should say rather, for your work and your nature represent a revelation of that god, and you will not be surprised to find the classical philologist who is such a zealous admirer of the gods among your well-wishers. You will be aware of *this* relationship too—how could you with your Hermetic nature not be aware of any relationship, however well hidden?—and thus you will not find it extravagent if I account your work a gift of the gods, one for which I am grateful to you and, through you, to the god Hermes, and ask him to grant you the wish that Horace, another *vir Mercurialis* [devotee of Mercury], asked for himself:

pingue pecus domino facias et cetera praeter
ingenium, utque soles, custos ei maximus adsis!

["Make fat the master's cattle and all else except his head, and as always, remain his chief protector"—Horace, *Satires,* II. 6, ll. 14–15].

3. This was received by all the well-wishers who had contributed to the attractive gift box that Mann's publisher, Gottfried Bermann Fischer, presented to him for his sixtieth birthday.

Mann to Kerényi

Küsnacht, September 29, 1935

Again, I find it marvelously interesting, significant, and stimulating,[1] dear Herr Professor. Many thanks! One should indeed read Otto's book,[2] but then again, it seems to me that it is not necessary, since in some respects your essay provides even more than the book. Incredible, how well this serves my purpose, for I am just now at work on the passion of Potiphar's wife, stylized in the manner of Dionysus and of the maenads.[3] You will certainly find traces of your study in the novel. If only it were completed. I am not coming to Budapest this year, and have declined all temptations to travel, in order to work.

Cordially,
Thomas Mann

1. "Gedanken über Dionysos," *Studi e materiali di storia delle religioni,* 11 (1935), 11–40.

2. *Dionysos, Mythos und Kultus* (Frankfort on the Main, 1933), the subject of my "reflections" in "Gedanken über Dionysos."

[3.] See *Joseph in Egypt,* chapters vi and vii (*Joseph and His Brothers,* pp. 667 ff; *GW,* V, 1004 ff.). For specific parallels between these chapters and Kerényi's essay see Dierks, *Studien,* pp. 266 ff.

Mann to Kerényi

Küsnacht-Zurich, March 2, 1936

Dear Herr Professor,

My thanks for the lovely, thoughtful lecture![1] I hope to see you in early summer, for if I can somehow do so, I want to take part in the meetings of the Comité des Lettres et des Arts in Budapest at the beginning of June. Naturally, there are all sorts of other temptations and almost obligations to travel: Vienna, Russia, even Argentina (PEN Club Congress). And meanwhile the third volume of *Joseph,* which should appear in the spring, is not quite ready, although it only goes up to the second journey into the "pit" and so does not yet bring the conclusion.

Yours sincerely,
T. M.

1. "Landschaft und Geist," *Die Welt als Geschichte,* 1 (1936); and in *Apollon.*

Mann to Kerényi

Küsnacht-Zurich, July 15, 1936

Dear Herr Professor,

I am very grateful that you have again added such an admirable piece[1] to my already rich collection of Kerényi writings. The fact that the late, not so blessed Wilamowitz does not fare too well in it is only a satisfaction of a secondary order. (I have never been able to bear this vain phantom and have always been astonished that he even dared to open his mouth after his attack on Nietzsche. He was, after all, a type of male Kundry; he had "laughed." He may have remained a great scholar to the end, but as a *thinker* he had lost any standing whatever.)[2]

The essay on Orpheus is again of the greatest interest. Wholly new for me was the connection to nirvana in "I escaped the sorrowful, painful circle." Page 11 shows how much the Platonic comes through in Schopenhauer: "Soul" (Will) = "Life." And then a great deal touching on Nietzsche; for that reason the whole analysis or specification of the Orphic, including the name of the "solitary," was particularly engrossing to me, and also the reference to the "wild high mountains" as Dionysian landscape.[3] This essay is among those things I have laid aside to read again when I am in earnest about the essay on Nietzsche, a subject that I have long contemplated and that lies most decidedly in my path.

In recent days you have been close to my work, and it has been close to you. I am, in fact, at work on an incantation scene at the end of *Joseph,* III [*Joseph in Egypt*], in which I utilize without any embarrassment your commentary on Sophron's mime of the women.[4] Anachronism no longer bothers me in the least—as a matter of fact, this was already so in the earlier volumes. In the third volume, Egyptian, Jewish, Greek, even medieval elements, both linguistic and mythological, make a colorful mixture. I have increasingly come to consider the whole as a *linguistic* product first of all, one to which all possible spheres must pay tribute and deliver materials.

Is it really true that you will take a look at the Hungarian translation of *J.i.E.?* This would, of course, be of great importance to me. And I would be especially grateful to know your impressions of those parts of the book that you have read.

With warmest greetings,

Sincerely yours,
Thomas Mann

1. "Orphische Seele," in *Gedenkschrift für Akos von Pauler* (Berlin, 1936). The most important material is also in *Pythagoras und Orpheus,* Albae Vigiliae, N.S. IX (3d, augmented ed.; Zurich, 1950), pp. 11–45 (*HSF,* pp. 15–51).

[2.] In Richard Wagner's opera *Parsifal,* Kundry, a sorceress in the guise of a lovely young woman, attempts to seduce Parsifal, but her mad laugh reveals her true nature in spite of herself.

[3.] Mann's references are to the original version of the essay in *Gedenkschrift für Akos von Pauler,* which could not be consulted. Corresponding passages in the essay "Pythagoras und Orpheus" in *HSF* are on pp. 45, 36–37, and 39. "I escaped the sorrowful, painful circle" ("Ich entflog dem traurigen schmerzhaften Kreise") is quoted from Otto Kern, *Orphicorum fragmenta* (Berlin, 1922), No. 32 c 6, according to Thomas Mann, *Briefe, 1889–1936,* ed. Erika Mann (Frankfort on the Main, 1961), p. 536.

4. See Kerényi to Mann, December 31, 1934, note 1.

Kerényi to Mann

Siófok, [Hungary], September 18, 1936

Dear, honored Herr Doctor,

I took with me your *Joseph in Egypt*—the German text and the proofs of the Hungarian translation up to the beginning of the second year of suffering—as I traveled from Val Camonica in the Brescian Alps, an area so rich in prehistoric and ancient cave paintings, through Porto Venere, that stern and lovely aphrodisiac region, to the isle of the sirens, Capri. (I think that if, after *The Magic Mountain,* you had not undertaken that grandiose venture into the mythological, "The Magic Island" would have had to follow the novel on Davos, with a picture of the total, blissful self-annihilation of that part of Hans Castorp's bourgeois society which had survived the war.) My trip was necessarily an educational one, as are all "Italian Journeys"[1] for us, but it was at the same time my honeymoon, and now, already halfway back home, I can finally give you my impressions of what I have read, impressions interwoven with the most enchanting, if not always clear, recollections.

There is less, of course, to say about the translation. It is good and can even be called artistic. It is a great thing that such translations of novels are even possible, especially when a novel is so much a "linguistic product" as *Joseph*. The "language" with which you work really moves on a deeper level than the merely *phonetic;* it is, so to speak, wholly transparent, since it can give expression to simply *everything* and yet make one feel that you only allow everything *to emerge into expression.* I had the same feeling of hearing "language" in itself during the lecture of a Spanish guide whom I heard by chance in St. Ambrogio in Milan. I apprehended nothing *disagreeable* but also *nothing agreeable* in a phonetic sense that stood in the way of my understanding *everything,* although— or because—I was not aware for a long time *what* language I was hearing. In this state of perfection language can wholly disappear, but without being muted—on the contrary, it is now as fluent as possible. Another form of perfection is of a material type, where the senses are affected in a most agreeable manner, as is often the case with Italian. *Your* language, however, is the most transparent, the most immaterial of substances, and perhaps for that reason so rewarding to translate.

And then again, it is precisely in this kind of language that everything depends on the content—so, at least, it would appear to someone for whom its essence lay in its transparency. Only when one has mastered the Egyptian material as you have can one speak this language. But of course that is an error. In that case the leading Egyptologists would also be the outstanding masters of language, and that is hardly true. Obviously, if works like your *Joseph in Egypt* are to come into being, a power of language must be added to the command of the material. To say this and not elucidate further what "power of language" means in this case would be trivial—and thus again an error.

For it is remarkable how much more you, who after all possess no professional credentials but only a "power of language" (and wish to have it no other way), are *really able* to say about Egyptian matters than the mere professionals! I say this not as an Egyptologist—which I am even less than you are—but as someone who likes to read something that, going beyond the bare data, gives a sense of the Egyptian essence, in the religious sphere for example. One of my best students is an Egyptologist, at the moment working in the Louvre, and he complains bitterly about an insensitivity to the essentials in even the best-trained professionals. I can understand this all too well. But he will certainly have nothing to complain of when he has read your *Joseph in Egypt;* on the contrary, he will become more aware of individual problems, of what is still not knowable in a scholarly form. The success of the whole will amaze him, and from the "re-creations"—like the dialogue of Huy and Tuy or the dying words of Mont-kaw (I admire both of these most, perhaps, of what I have read so far)—he will certainly learn something of the essence of Egypt.

What kind of "language" is this, I am compelled to ask, which allows precisely what is essential, what is universally true, to shine forth with such clarity? (I trust you will forgive me this unintentional "disquisition" on "the essence of language in Thomas Mann," especially since, as you will see immediately, it involves something altogether general, extending far beyond the individual manifestation.) For I am not inclined to separate "power of language" from an ability to perceive essentials or "intuition." It is through individuals thus possessed of the "power of language" that the reality of the universe expresses itself, and the more endowed one is in this respect, the more able one will be to speak of reality. The unfolding of this power of language—which is not an individual endowment but a force that extends over generations and epochs, in fact requires them, until, having attained its fullest development, it regresses once more—this unfolding is essentially identical with the self-revelation of the cosmos, of universal reality.

One of the great experiences of my youth was reading [Georg Moritz] Ebers' *Uarda* [1877]. In looking back now on that in every sense outdated historical novel, how much greater is the power of expression I find in *Joseph*. And this power of expression is to be explained, not merely in terms of an individual artistic capacity that goes far beyond Ebers', but also by the fact that today there *exists* in principle the capacity of expressing things which were totally concealed in Ebers' time. One notes with astonishment from your Αἰγύπτιοι λόγοι[2] how far we have advanced in the disciplines of ethnology, mythology, archaeology, and philology—not because you are dependent on these disciplines (you are much less, I think, than Ebers was), but because the greatest artistry and the peak of a general, not individual, maturity of the spirit always coincide.

In depicting the beauty of Petepre's[3] wife your allusions to the swan showed me how such a "maturity of the spirit" manifests itself clearly in the most varied, often even opposing, personalities and discloses in this manner the ripened, new capacity. I *had* to think of the recurrence of the Leda myth in D. H. Lawrence's poems, not on account of the theme itself but because of the awakening, as it were, of a feeling for the essential quality of the swan—a quality that is not merely decorative, as in rococo artists and still in Richard Wagner (how would he have dared otherwise to make of the *swan* a

[71]

theatrical *machine!*), but that is truly a universal essence and can thus enter into a significant relationship with the essence of the feminine. It seems to me that here, and in fact in the whole work, you have definitively overcome the essentially disintegrating mode of analysis of Freudianism, in favor of a view of organic universal essences, such as that of the swan or of the aquatic birds, essences that are not susceptible to further analysis. (Unfortunately, I do not know your lecture on Freud,[4] and by "overcoming" I mean completely taking possession of a position, *including* mastering the step that goes beyond it.) In other words, you have indicated a return to the essentially perceptible surface of the world, with its countless natural and meaningful, ultimately even divine, forms: creatures of the swamp or swan or Mut-en-emet,[5] this newborn sister of Euripedes' Phaedra. You have fashioned her in a paradigmatic manner, without Freudianism, naturally and classically, like the heroine of a Greek tragedy, worthy to stand beside Goethe's Iphigenia.

So, at least, I judge from what I have read thus far of her, up to the beginning of the second year of her passion.

I sense that what concerns me especially has yet to follow, but I did not want to delay answering your letter, for which I thank you warmly. I am in complete agreement with what you say about Nietzsche and Wilamowitz.

With most devoted greetings,

Yours,
Karl Kerényi

[1.] An allusion to Goethe's *Italienische Reise* (1816–1817).

2. "Egyptian tales."

[3.] The Egyptian form of Potiphar. See *Joseph and His Brothers,* p. 544 (*GW,* IV, 809). See further Mann's discussion of Biblical names in *Pariser Rechenschaft* (*GW,* XI, 56 f.).

[4.] See Mann to Kerényi, October 7, 1936, note 1.

[5.] Potiphar's wife.

Mann to Kerényi

Dear Herr Professor,

In my dedication to the Freud lecture[1] I sought to express my gratitude and to show how responsive I am to your judicious and subtle letter on the third part of *Joseph*. Now you reply by putting me in your debt once more with your lovely study on *religio*,[2] in which, incidentally, you correct a section of that lecture with masterful learning—or rather, you put the seriousness of scholarship in the place of a half-playful etymology of convenience.[3] There is probably little more than this to my "interpretation" of the word *religio*, through which I wanted to indicate the rather daring and spiritually probably somewhat shocking definition of the "covenant" as an act of mutual aid between God and man for the purpose of achieving the holy—a double process for which God requires man as much as the latter does Him. This idea has a strong humoristic coloring, as does all the theology in *Joseph*. And the humoristic is peculiar in that it is not wholly lacking in seriousness but at the same time does not want to be held strictly to the letter: rather, it is a kind of truthful jest that certainly has a rightful place even though it does not compete with actual scholarship. For this reason my pleasure in the rich, factual findings of your work are quite unclouded by a guilty conscience. It is admirable that with each of your contributions, each choice of a problem, you are able to hit upon something really interesting —at least to me, which indicates a certain pre-established friendship between our spheres. The stimulation and personal satisfaction I have gotten from this essay are yet another testimony of this. What I find particularly appealing here is a cer-

[73]

tain preference for the "secularization" of the concept of religion, for its psychological conversion into the profane spheres of morality and the soul. Religion as the opposite of negligence and disregard, as taking care, respecting, considering, conscience, as a *vigilant* attitude,[4] indeed as *metus*,[5] and finally as a concerned, attentive receptivity to the movements of the universal spirit—what more can I wish? Suddenly I find it legitimate to call myself a religious individual, a self-estimate which, in "prudence," I would otherwise hardly dare to make.

Joseph in Egypt should appear in the middle of the month. May you still find some pleasure in the concluding sections! My conscience is by no means "clear," and yet it seems to me that with this volume something special, something that is in a new manner conducive to human cheer has come into the world.

Sincerely yours,
Thomas Mann

[1.] *Freud und die Zukunft* (Vienna, 1936; *GW,* IX) ("Freud and the Future," in *Essays of Three Decades*). Mann's dedication, reproduced in facsimile in the German edition, p. 73, may be translated as follows:

> Karl Kerényi, To the expert, the true initiate, once again in sincere attachment for his remarkable letter concerning Joseph.
> Küsnacht, September 29, 1936
>
> Thomas Mann.

2. "Eulabeia," *Byzantinisch-neugriechische Jahrbücher,* 8 (1931), 306–316; given in return for *Freud und die Zukunft*.

3. The mistaken derivation of *religio* from *ligare* (to attach) was the traditional one. Thomas Mann had probably kept it from his school days.

4. Thus in the essay about *eulabeia* (circumspection, care), "piety" is equivalent to "vigilance."

5. "Fear."

Kerényi to Mann

Dear, honored Herr Doctor,

I am again at Lake Balaton, as when I wrote you my last
long letter in September, and I ask your indulgence for having
brought my typewriter with me but leaving my writing paper
at home. Please do not take offense at this sort of letter; I do
feel, at any rate, now, for the first time since September, the
festive mood that I require, that is connected with my writing
to you. You were absolutely right to speak in your Freud lecture of the poet as the festive individual *kat' exochén* [pre-
eminently]: the essence of festivity, of ceremony, is, in my
view, a stilling of the course of the world so that eternal forms
may reveal themselves and, by this revelation, expand the
moment into an arrested eternity. That spiritual reality whose
temporal expression is "ceremony" and whose objective content is "eternal forms" was called *theoria* by the Greeks and is
"contemplation" to us; and one should be both ceremonial
and contemplative in approaching the poet, whether in a personal or impersonal capacity . . .

And here I may briefly remark how well we understand each
other precisely regarding the concept of "religion"! You spoke,
in that lovely letter on the subject, of your preference for a
secularization of the concept of religion. "Secularization," however, applies only in terms of the present-day situation of the
saeculum [worldly existence], which has been defined by Christianity as essentially irreligious. But if, instead of this tempor-
ally and historically designated *saeculum* we take the eternal as
a standard, if we accept the etymological meaning of *religio*[2]
as eternally valid for mankind, for as long, at least, as the pos-

sibility of human existence survives, then you are, simply and unequivocally, in possession of religion as such. And in this you as a poet stand close, not to the visionary and prophetic type, but to the type that observes and listens, which is akin to the scholarly. To hearken and reorient oneself is perhaps less than to perceive and transform oneself, but it is religious in the truest sense of the word; it is already ceremonial, even if not in such a carefree, festive spirit as is proper in major devotional ceremonies; but one's concern is already directed toward the eternal and not toward ordinary, transient existence. I have a similar conception of the *religio Academici,* which I intend to elaborate in published form soon[3]—that is, for the few who still (or already) possess a feeling for the sort of learning that testifies to a purified and attentive religiosity. You will understand these words if anyone does—the product of a very somber mood, I regret to say.

I would actually like to say something more about *Joseph in Egypt.* When I wrote the last letter about it, Mut was revealing to the reader all her Iphigenia-like beauty. The dissolution came only later, and I find it most ingenious how you have invested this dissolution with an oriental atmosphere—consciously and very artfully, for example, in "The Ladies' Party" —so that the Grecian figure is not utterly decomposed but, as it were, *melts away.* Nothing in the world has so much the taste and feel of melting as the "painful tongue." The suggestion of maenad, on the one hand, and of slut, on the other, in the new, liquefied figure of Potiphar's wife reveals two possibilities of the feminine, one more characteristic of antiquity and the other of the Middle Ages; but you are right to suggest the two, since they are both realizations of eternal forms—eternal, as I remarked earlier, insofar as human existence, even as a possibility, survives. For this reason I do not find anachronistic the showing of the bitch together with a negro priestess, and in an Egyptian milieu. On the contrary, this confirms my interpretation of the Greek Hekate as an eternal form with unending potency, who is involved here too, participating, as it were, in the structure of an endless feminine destiny. Or to put it more personally: the confirmation for me lies in the fact that *you* have indicated this structural pattern in Mut's destiny by the figure of the bitch.

And then, the five reasons for Joseph's chastity gave me much to think about. How remarkable that Hippolytus' reason (I think of Hyppolytus as the friend and devotee of Artemis) does not appear among them. It is barely intimated in the significant sentence: "Yet even the modern world might have to concede the possible existence of another kind: a blithe, even supercilious chastity."[4] The figure of Enkidu was familiar in the ancient Orient—Gilgamesh's companion—who, like one of the elements, lived invincible among the creatures of the forest as long as he remained chaste. When he lost his purity, the animals abhorred him. The divine purity of wild nature and of those who are a part of it is something totally different (altogether heathen!) from the bridal purity of Joseph before the countenance of *his* God. If at first I regretted that Hippolytus' qualities were not made prominent enough in the figure of Joseph, I was content in the end and recognize here too *the luck of the great artist*.

Since this is in any case a New Year's letter, let me close with my good wishes.

Most sincerely yours,
Karl Kerényi

My new Budapest address (since I only remain here until the New Year): I. Kutvölgyi-ut 42 b.

[1.] Typewritten.
[2.] As "scrupulous carefulness," according to Kerényi in *The Religion of the Greeks and Romans* (*Die antike Religion*), p. 97.
   3. "Religio Academici" ("The Religiosity of the Academic") was given

as a lecture at the Doorner Arbeitsgemeinschaft and was first published in the Hungarian periodical *Pannonia*, 4 (1938), 3–12. It was incorporated in *La religione antica* (Bologna, 1939) and in *Die antike Religion* (*The Religion of the Greeks and Romans*, pp. 154–162).

[4.] *Joseph and His Brothers*, p. 751 (*GW*, V, 1137).

Mann to Kerényi

Küsnacht-Zurich, May 4, 1937

Dear Herr Professor,

I have just returned from New York, rather exhausted and afflicted with a painful neuralgia (sciatica) in the left leg, after twelve days of lectures, dinners, and "meeting-speeches"[1]—a somewhat hectic pace for a man of my years. I find your book here in the mail that has accumulated.[2] Let me straightaway, as well as I can, as briefly as I may, *thank* you for the kind present! It is a true pleasure for me to have these essays, a store of learning and intuition, conveniently compiled in a volume. How often will I look into it, and particularly when I am working again on *Joseph!* The study about Sophron leaves me still with an amused conscience . . . I am waiting for the first critic to notice where I got the chapter "The Bitch" in the third volume of *Joseph*. It will have to come one day.[3]

My contact with America, where I have many friends, has been strengthened. We are seriously considering the idea of spending a part of each year there in the future. Such a distancing from Europe would be immensely beneficial to my serenity and freedom of mind.

I find it strange to experience this beloved season of blossoming accompanied by so many bodily pains as I have now.

[78]

There is probably nothing serious in this. If Pyramidon[4] and warm compresses do not help, I will have to find a bath cure. At the same time there is much to be done with the small novel on Goethe [*The Beloved Returns*] and the periodical *Mass und Wert* that has been founded here; my name is to appear as publisher—this is a very problematic function that I have undertaken. Have I asked you yet for a contribution? Then let me do so now.

Yours cordially,
Thomas Mann

[1.] In the German edition, "meeting-speeches" is in English.

2. The first edition of *Apollon* (Vienna, 1937).

[3.] Dierks, *Studien,* pp. 206 and 268, specifies the sources, notably Kerényi's "Sophron oder der griechische Naturalismus" (see Kerényi to Mann, December 31, 1934, note 1) and Apuleius' novel *The Golden Ass* (2d century, A.D.).

[4.] A medication.

Mann to Kerényi

Küsnacht-Zurich, September 1, 1937

Dear Herr Professor,

Thank you for your address[1] and for your manuscript.[2] I for my part read it with great interest and can only hope that our editor, who now has it, will not find it too much outside the scope and aims of our periodical.

We will definitely still be here until the 15th, going then to Tessin. You will find us in Küsnacht through the 14th and be most welcome here.

Sincerely yours,
Thomas Mann

1. In England, at the Warburg Instiute, London S.W. 7. I had notified him of our intended visit to Küsnacht.

2. "Die religiöse Idee des Nichtseins." During my visit to Küsnacht in September 1937, I withdrew the essay from *Mass und Wert,* whose editor, in truth, showed little enthusiasm for it. It appears as an epilogue in my book *Die antike Religion.*

Mann to Kerényi

Küsnacht-Zurich, November 13, 1937

Dear Herr Professor,

Splendid, your long review of Pettazzoni's book[1]—most interesting. My warm thanks! I too have once again been hard at work on "myth" in recent days. I am finishing a lecture to be given next week at the university on Wagner's *Ring des Nibelungen* on the occasion of a complete performance at the Stadttheater. Cordial greetings to your lovely wife, whose visit we keep in friendliest memory.

Sincerely yours,
Thomas Mann

1. Raffaele Pettazzoni, *La confessione dei peccati,* I–III (Bologna, 1928–1936). My critical study entitled "Gedanken über Sündenbekenntnis" appeared in *Die Welt als Geschichte,* 3 (1937), 392–398.

Mann to Kerényi

Küsnacht-Zurich, July 13, 1938

Dear Herr Professor,

These are undoubtedly very tardy thanks for your engrossing Catullus essay.[1] It has been well worth saving; I found it here in a great mass of mail on returning from almost half a year in America.

This new and intensive contact with America has brought with it changes in my life. Our present stay here is only in the nature of a visit. In the middle of September we sail once more in order to settle in Princeton, New Jersey, where I have entered into a firm commitment as "lecturer in the humanities" at the university. Actually, this post will not seriously stand in the way of my own work. Also, this change of residence is not to be considered as a real separation from Europe. If the situation allows it—you know what is meant—we intend to spend a few months every year on the old continent.

May you get through these days and this history in safety and with good fortune!

Sincerely yours,
Thomas Mann

1. In *Pester Lloyd,* June 5, 1938; reprinted in *Apollon,* second and subsequent editions.

Mann to Kerényi

Küsnacht-Zurich, September 9, 1938

Dear Herr Professor,

My cordial thanks! Everything has arrived in good order, particularly the "Papyri,"[1] which I shall read at leisure on board ship. The movers have been here. That's over now. But actually we are already gone and only haunt these rooms with their bare bookcases like floating bodies or ships without ballast rocking in the waves. On the 17th we begin our rocking in earnest.

My "program" for Princeton—good heavens, it's not to be

taken so seriously. The important point is that I live and work there. Further, I am to give four or five lectures in the course of the academic year on whatever I wish: on *Faust,* on Goethe otherwise, on Schopenhauer, Wagner, or Freud. I am even to expatiate now and then on my own *Magic Mountain.* But that is the extent of it. They are friendly and want to make it easy for me, and when I ask for instructions, I am always urged not to take things so seriously. All of which doesn't exclude my doing my part as well as I can and not merely as well as may be necessary.

Here is my address: Princeton, N.J., 65 Stockton Street, U.S.A. It's an attractive house, with much greenery about, which we had already rented when we were there in June, and it's good to know that New York is only an hour away and Philadelphia not much more. Everything will be all right once my books arrive; the desk is set up, and the help, a negro couple, is learning how we like our food. That an ocean lies between me and the liberation of the Sudeten Germans will, I suppose, facilitate the completion of *The Beloved Returns* so that I may again tell the tale of the dismembered and resurrected Joseph. It will, after all, be a strange and delightful experience to see this gigantic jest completed one day. What is really strange and delightful, it seems, is death. For one is always striving and wishing to get finished without noticing that in essence one strives for the sake of *being* finished and for death.

Visit us one day soon there in the robust realm of the dead!

Sincerely yours,

Thomas Mann

1. "Die Papyri und das Problem des griechischen Romans," in *Actes du Ve Congrès international de Papyrologie* (1938), and in *Apollon,* second and subsequent editions.

Mann to Kerényi

Dear Herr Professor,

I read your lovely essay on the birth of Helen[2] yesterday on the train to New York. I can not tell you how much this one, too, of your works has stimulated, enriched, and moved me. The sphere of your investigations has a magical power of attraction for me, and the relationships you disclose—this mysterious unity of Helen, Nemesis, and Aphrodite—have occupied and entertained me in a most spirited way ever since you gave me a glimpse of them. After reading something like this, I always wish that I were again on *Joseph,* which you could aid more directly than my present undertaking. But actually I can not guarantee that the reading of your essay will not make itself felt in the Goethe novel [*The Beloved Returns*] as well, since in the end it will not get along entirely without Helen. That would be a task for you one day: to write about Goethe's conception of Helen. The way in which the spirit of antiquity mixes here with that of the rococo and gallantry has in it something wholly unique and delightfully unsanctioned, something that has never yet, as far as I know, been analyzed with the capacities you possess.

In reading your essay I was reminded of the encounters Goethe had with your deceased colleague the mythologist Creuzer, about which one may read in Biedermann's *Gespräche.*[3] Creuzer had a conversation with Goethe in Heidelberg in 1815 about the symbolic interpretation of figures and stories from Greek mythology, a conversation that reveals in the strongest terms Goethe's deep interest in these matters. For me, the mythological in Goethe, especially in the "Classical

Walpurgis Night," has always been the bridge that leads from
him to [Richard] Wagner, who adored precisely this part of
Faust and used to read aloud from it during his last days in
Venice, to frequent cries of admiration from those about him.

We are well adjusted now to this new environment. The
external circumstances were favorable, the inner difficult; for
I need hardly say that the events in Europe have imposed new
burdens and anxieties. I do not want to go into that; I have
given vent to my feelings in a short essay, *Dieser Friede*[4] [*This
Peace*], which has appeared in English too and of which many
thousand copies have already been distributed here. The situation in Hungary is hardly clear to me. Perhaps I could have at
least some indications about that from you. When will we see
each other again? The way to Budapest is cut off for me, the
way to Europe itself not yet, I trust; and Switzerland in the
summer would be the best meeting place—assuming, indeed,
that your path will not eventually bring you across the ocean.

Keep well. My warmest thanks once more for the intellectual joy you have again given me, and do not fail to keep me
abreast of your work in the future.

Very sincerely yours,
Thomas Mann

P.S. I recently held my first two lectures here, which were
public. They dealt with Goethe's *Faust* and brought me much
friendly reaction from young and old alike.

[1.] Typewritten.

2. Thomas Mann received a copy prepared for him at Doorn, where
the lecture was given. "Die Geburt der Helena" was first published in
the Dutch periodical *Mnemosyne,* 3d series, 7 (1939), 161–179; subsequently in *Die Geburt der Helena samt humanistischen Schriften aus
den Jahren 1943–1945,* Albae Vigilae, N.S. III (Zurich, 1945); and in
HSF, pp. 52–67.

[3.] *Goethe's Gespräche,* ed. Flodoard von Biedermann (5 vols.; Leipzig, 1909–1911). Georg Friedrich Creuzer (1771–1858) was a philo-

logist and archaeologist whose major work was *Symbolik und Mythologie der alten Völker, besonders der Griechen* (1810–1812).

[4.] Stockholm, 1938 (*GW*, XII, 829–845) (*This Peace* [New York, 1938]).

Kerényi to Mann

Siófok, December 24, 1938

Dear, honored Herr Professor,

Your friendly words have hitherto always supported me at decisive junctures—points I had reached by the methods of scholarship but where these alone no longer sufficed. The response of a great intellect and artist was far more valuable than mere scholarly endorsement. But your last letter was even more important to me than any before, and I am all the more grateful to you for it. You have demonstrated in the kindest manner your full understanding of the essay on Helen. For me this essay signifies a decisive step, not only in scholarly but in personal terms: it is a breakthrough in fulfilling what I was perhaps born for—to establish the science of the great mythologies. When you called me a "mythologist" years ago in your study on *Don Quixote*,[1] you saw the direction the intellect in me had taken much more clearly than I saw it myself. It is not for nothing that you now mention Creuzer's relations to Goethe. And you surely know too why Creuzer's mythology was wholly mistaken: because he was incapable of comprehending symbolism in the Goethian sense. There is much I could say about the newer science of mythology, that disintegration of myth into language and legend devoid of any spiritual substance. W. F. Otto, the only exception among the philologists, is rather a theologian (in the fundamental sense of the word) than a mythologist, and my own first breakthrough ten years ago was precisely to "theology" in that sense. Why

[85]

have I been collecting scholarly tools for twenty years, and why did I pursue Indology even in my youth, along with classical philology, and why have I flirted with oriental as well as Norse and various exotic studies, if not for what I now face: the great science of mythology itself? Most of my preparations have been made in accordance with instinct and even destiny. My destiny brought me to Frobenius,[2] that protean natural spirit of ethnological studies, during the last years of his life, when he was already totally involved in collecting materials for his massive science of universal mythology. He died with the melancholy knowledge that his collection had not progressed even far enough to be utilized without danger. This fall, as I came through Frankfort from Holland, where I had given the Helen lecture, I leafed through the immense collection of mythological extracts he had left behind, and I realized that I must venture at my own risk, with complete involvement, into the sources of the great mythologies that lie beyond classical antiquity. Since then I have familiarized myself with the mythological world of the Finno-Ugric tribes, for which my knowledge of Hungarian has been a great help. These studies are already useful in the book I am working on now, entitled *Prometheus,* on the question of the Titans. (The lecture on Helen will be a chapter in it.)[3] What I still absolutely require is America, with its splendid collections and studies of Indian mythology, about which Frobenius always spoke enthusiastically. I also need to study the older American period. But that is not the only reason why America would be important for me. If you out there already feel a disquieting pressure, of those "burdens and anxieties" of the spirit of which you write, how much more do I feel it, who now in my early forties sense both a potential for the greatest intellectual accomplishment and the prospect of losing my means of existence. If the way to you—the way of the humanists, of which we spoke[4]—were opened up to me by the possibility of pursuing my work on mythology in America, then I would come immediately. But for the moment I see no such way. It may be possible to visit you if you come to Switzerland soon. And then we could speak of Goethe's Helen, whom I did not mention in my lecture only because she cannot, of course, be briefly dealt with. If my destiny allows it, I shall be happy to follow your suggestion that I write about her, and then I would also say something about the "Classical Walpurgis Night" for which my knowledge of certain early mythologies qualifies me. Your new work *This Peace* has not yet arrived. Your letter will reach me via my Budapest address (Kutvölgyi-ut 42b).

I close with the best wishes for the New Year to yourself and your family, also from my wife.

Very sincerely yours,
Karl Kerényi

1. In *Leiden und Grösse der Meister, GW,* IX, 454 (*Essays of Three Decades,* p. 448).

[2.] Leo Frobenius (1873–1938), German explorer and ethnologist, the foremost authority of his time on prehistoric art.

3. *Prometheus* became, in fact, a small book. See Mann to Kerényi, June 14, 1946, note 2. The lecture on Helen retained its original form. See Mann to Kerényi, December 6, 1938, note 2.

4. Refers to a conversation in Küsnacht in 1937 in which the mission of the intellectuals who emigrated to America was compared to the role of the Greek scholars who, after the fall of Constantinople, fled to Italy.

Mann to Kerényi

Princeton, February 16, 1939

Dear Professor Kerényi,

I received your Christmas letter twice and read your essay on festival[1] twice—are you content? I need not say, and could hardly do so, how much at home I feel in this piece of yours, which I consider among the finest you have written—perhaps I would give it the palm altogether, seduced as I am by its close ties to all the things that afford me refreshment and relief from the miserable stupidity and mediocrity of public affairs. My judgment, then, has a personal slant, but I seriously think that the essay has an outstanding place among your productions and represents a higher, freer stage, not only in its stylistic qualities but also in its elegant presentation of the argument. This may be related to the "breakthrough" to a higher and wider scholarly sphere of which you spoke, though I hardly see it as a breakthrough, since I have long considered you a more or less conscious member of that circle in which my artistic intuition allows me to play a dilettante role.

You can imagine how often I had to think of *Joseph* as I read you. Festival, in the sense of a mythical ceremony, a recurrence, at once cheerful and serious, of a primal event, is in fact virtually *the* fundamental theme of my novel, and its hero is once explicitly called "Joseph-em-heb"—"Joseph in the Feast." I might have felt a longing for my book, as happens so often when I read something pertinent. But nothing of the sort was needed, since your essay aroused a good many ideas that are also related to my present intellectual preoccupation, the Goethe novel. Isn't it too, finally, "mythology"? In short, much that you write struck me as singularly familiar: your remarks about the loss of life in living through repetition, and about the residue of a creative element in the process of repetition; further, about the pronounced compatibility of vital and intellectual experience, of life and meaning. One of the major themes of *The Beloved Returns* is the repetition of life in a *spiritually enhanced* although also less vital form;[2] for the Hatem infatuation with Marianne Willemer involves just such a repetition of the Lotte experience. She is even called Jung.[3] The beloved is always young; but what is somewhat bewildering is that, alongside the ageless one, the Lotte who has grown old is also still here and presents herself.—Something like that.

I wish that I could be of help in your wish to come to America, that I might arrange an invitation. If you would indicate whom to approach, I'd be glad to try. Do you speak English?

The best to you and your wife!

Thomas Mann

1. "Vom Wesen des Festes," *Paideuma,* 1 (1938), 59 ff.; *Die antike Religion,* chapter ii.

[2]. *The Beloved Returns* (*Lotte in Weimar,* 1939) is the fictional reconstruction of a true episode in Goethe's life: the visit to Weimar in 1816 of the woman who more than forty years before had served as the model for the young heroine, Lotte, of Goethe's first novel, *The Sorrows of Young Werther* (1774).

[3.] Hatem is the name assumed by Goethe in certain poems of *West-östlicher Divan* (1819) addressed to Marianne von Willemer (nee Jung). Goethe was in his mid-sixties and Marianne in her early thirties in the period of their association.

Kerényi to Mann

Pécs (?), spring 1939

Dear, honored Professor Mann!

My warmest thanks for your friendly words in which you characterize my situation within a specific sphere of existence in ideal terms. It is somewhat more difficult for me to determine the actual state of affairs in which I find myself. You have undoubtedly guessed from the fact that I sent the same letter to you by two different routes how dismal matters were at the time. Not I alone but also other thinking and feeling children of our country—and not the worst—sensed the imminence of an abyss. Not even the possibility of combat for

[89]

the human and truly Hungarian national values seemed to remain open. I *could not help* thinking of great Hungarian emigrants—not that I want to compare myself with them—such as Kossuth in America or my namesake, the poet Kerényi, who died in Iowa after the Hungarian war of independence, or my German compatriot Lenau.[1] And then there was also the purely practical aspect of which I spoke in my letter: the possibility of extending my mythological horizon by means of the collections in ethnology and early American archaeology to be found there.

At the moment the situation is somewhat better. I do not know whether I will have to share the fate of my namesake or not. If so, I will do it not simply as *homo humanus* [a member of the human race] but also as *Romanus* [a Roman], that is, as a citizen of a still free nation. But the practical need to pursue studies in America remains for me independent of that. And I can imagine the possibility that aid may come from that side of the world to help me lay a new foundation for the science of mythology—an idea that has taken hold of me and become a compelling intellectual task. For perhaps there in America they begin to sense, through you and your *Joseph,* what "myth" is in its unadulterated, apolitical, primordial, festive sense, pure and profound like philosophy and music at once. Only the preparatory work, collecting and arranging, concerns me now, not presentation. It would also take some months of long practice in an English or American setting to allow my written English to develop into a living language.

One of my best friends may come to Princeton during these days, the art historian Karl von Tolnay [b. 1899]. I hope you will allow him to visit you. He has not only written the best books available about Breughel, Hieronymus Bosch, and the van Eyck brothers (his unpublished work on Michelangelo will be *the* book on the subject), but he is also an upright person, a true and fearless champion of his discipline and of humanity.

I hope soon to be able to send you a study, "What Is Mythology?"[2] You will see therein how thankful I am for your stimulation in clarifying the basic concepts; even more, for providing the best formulations yet of the relation between myth and life. I thank you, not only for the intellectual support your works and letters have given me, but now also for your interest in my future. I await what this future may bring strengthened by your concern for me.

Ever yours,
Karl Kerényi

[1.] Lajos Kossuth (1802–1894), patriot and leader in the revolution of 1848–1849, was exiled from Hungary after 1849. Friedrich Kerényi could not be further identified. Nikolaus Lenau (1802–1850), German poet of Hungarian birth, spent two years establishing a farm in Pennsylvania but then returned to Europe.

2. See Introduction, note 40.

Mann to Kerényi

Noordwijk aan Zee (Holland), August 2, 1939

Dear Herr Professor,

Your essay "What Is Mythology?"[1] is most interesting. I have carefully preserved it, well marked up, until I can again take up the Joseph legend, at which time it will serve, along with your other works, to awaken and stimulate a mythical mood.

That time no longer seems distant. We were decidedly well advised to spend the first part of our European vacation here. It is a magnificent location. I have appreciably recovered from the hardships of the American winter, and during this process

I was so active mornings in my cabin on the beach that I entertained the fantastic hope of still finishing the Goethe novel (of which you may have seen some fragments in *Mass und Wert*) by the fall deadline, even if I only write the final chapter in October, after our return "home." We leave here the day after tomorrow to spend two weeks in Zurich for conferences with my publisher and with my second son, who has assumed editorship of the periodical; then to London to visit my second daughter, who is married there, and finally to Stockholm where I must be a delegate of the German section to the PEN Club Congress. Also, there will be some matters to discuss there with Dr. [Gottfried] Bermann Fischer about re-issuing the edition of my works, which is no longer available in German, as the Stockholmer Gesamt-Ausgabe.[2] Then, in the latter half of September comes the return to our new home, where we have received our "first papers," and where I am an honorary doctor of no less than 6 universities, as well as corresponding member of the Academy of Arts and Sciences. These are pleasant anchors that they have allowed me to cast in that soil, where after all it would no longer be possible for me to sink firm roots—not that I really have the wish.

You also seek to come across, and quite rightly, of course. In spite of a certain primitivity, lack of nerve, and simplicity, it is a proper, well-meaning country, with a positive longing for what is good and right. And though you will find class prejudice and blind conceit there, and even, as everywhere, a secret sympathy for Fascism that masquerades as concern for freedom and democracy, it is still a country where, as probably nowhere else today, the public feeling is on our side. In short, the general atmosphere would be a comfort to you too. Furthermore, your letter[3] reveals to me for the first time something of your personal situation, and I can therefore understand your wish all the better. How much I would like to be of service to you! It will hardly be possible to do anything from

Europe, but I have noted the address of the historian of religion at Harvard whom you know, and upon my return will try to make clear to him how stimulating your work would be for humanistic studies in America. But it may be that I will encounter some resistance, if not with Nock[4] then at some later stage, a resistance against foreign intruders that has made itself felt more and more there too . . .

Dear God, my *Faust* lectures were truly of the harmless sort, intended for boys. At least one can say that the "incommensurable" work was seen with tolerably fresh eyes—which may be called the American side of the affair. But I am tremendously curious about your study of the Neptune scenes in the "Classical Walpurgis Night." It is a shame I did not yet know it when I depicted Goethe, in an inner monologue, thinking of this project.[5] I found it quite remarkable in reading your essay on mythology to see how, through mutual support and aid, a kind of joint undertaking on a philosophy of myth has evolved between us, an undertaking in which the profit and learning, if not in all the essentials then certainly in all the particulars, have been on my side.

Sincerely yours,
Thomas Mann

1. See Introduction, note 40.

[2.] Although a number of editions of Mann's works between 1939 and 1958 bear the imprint "Stockholmer Gesamtausgabe der Werke von Thomas Mann," they do not constitute a complete edition nor were they all printed in Stockholm. See Hans Bürgin, *Das Werk Thomas Manns: Eine Bibliographie* (Frankfort on the Main, 1959), pp. 57–58. Gottfried Bermann Fischer was the son-in-law and successor of Mann's long-time publisher Samuel Fischer. Forced to liquidate his firm in Germany in 1935, Bermann Fischer re-established it in Austria in 1936 and then, driven out again, in Stockholm in 1938.

3. This letter has not yet been found.

[4.] Arthur Darby Nock (1902–1963), professor at Harvard.

[5.] See Introduction, note 16.

Kerényi to Mann

Budapest, [after Christmas ?] 1939

Dear, honored Herr Professor,

It is again the period between Christmas and the New Year, a cosmic turning point and a natural moment of rest, a time to pause and catch one's breath, which, for many years now, I have devoted to writing to those few individuals whom I cherish. To be sure, it is the Finns alone whom we poor Europeans have to thank for the pause this year. It is a true marathon in the north, the marathon of a people that stands just as close to *its* great epic, the *Kalevala,* as the Greek *marathon-omachoi*[1] stood to Homer. I hardly expected, while reading the *Kalevala* last winter—parts of it out loud—how much the nation of that great epic would be on our minds this winter, a source of anxiety and of unbelievable consolation too. If you wish to become acquainted with something truly mythological and on a level with the epic of the Biblical story of creation, something in which the author of the Joseph novel will find a world that is familiar and yet full of unexpected discoveries, I can only recommend that you read the *Kalevala.* You may find the German translation of [Anton] Schiefner passable; unfortunately we Hungarians do not understand Finnish either, but we possess an outstanding translation.

One of the fruits of my work on the *Kalevala* was a study of the "primordial child," which is a sequel both to the essay "What Is Mythology?" (an example of it) and to "Die Geburt der Helena" (the study of the "primordial woman"). It has appeared only in Hungarian, as the introduction to a bilingual edition of the Homeric "Hymn to Hermes"; I am now working on the German version.[2] I intend to publish it, to-

[94]

gether with "What Is Mythology?" and another essay that will state my position on C. G. Jung's theory of myths, in the series devoted to humanistic studies, Albae Vigiliae, of which I am editor. There are, however, great difficulties with my publisher, Pantheon in Amsterdam; I am pretty much at his mercy, though not bound to him. Could you recommend a publisher, in Switzerland or elsewhere, who would have some interest in my mythological subjects and would respect my intellectual freedom?

My most heartfelt thanks too for all that you wished to do for me over there. My longing for the fullest development is greater than ever, but I am also confident that this period is in fact a turning point. Let this be my New Year's wish too. And allow me again to recommend to you my friend Prof. Tolnay, the art historian in Princeton.

Yours sincerely,
Karl Kerényi

1. "Combatants at Marathon."
2. "Das Urkind in der Urzeit" (*HSF,* pp. 68–115) appeared later with a commentary by C. G. Jung in *Das göttliche Kind.* See Kerényi to Mann, November 15, 1940, note 2.

Mann to Kerényi

Princeton, October 25, 1940

Dear Professor Kerényi,

I have received your lovely essay on the "Classical Walpurgis Night."[1] It is for me the favorite of all your works—and how could it be otherwise, since I have long wished to see you deal with this subject? You have succeeded astonishingly well in making one sense Goethe's mythological disposition, his affinity for the "mystical" of antiquity, which underlies his *play*

[95]

with the sphere of myth and of mysteries, a play that is often light and mocking but that can nonetheless rise to a level of dignity and solemnity and that accounts for the fact that he was instinctively so far ahead of the mythologists, philologists, and archaeologists of his time. I was especially pleased to see that you too consider the marriage of Homunculus and Galatea—that is, the myth of the creation of man—a kind of exposition for the Helen act: in other words, an elaborate and grandiose scientific-poetic-mystical preparation for the appearance of the Beautiful. I do not know who brought this idea up first; but I would credit Goethe with it and *have* done so in the 7th chapter of *The Beloved Returns,* in that monologue which deals with the "Classical Walpurgis Night." I wonder if you have read the book? It is remarkable how our thoughts sometimes run along the same lines. I was almost astounded when I read the passage in your study dealing with that mystical idea of antiquity, the identity of mother and daughter (Demeter-Persephone). For that same morning, in working on one of the chapters of the new Joseph volume [*Joseph the Provider*], I had included an anecdote about someone who, without knowing who she is, falls in love with the daughter of a woman whom he had loved as a young girl twenty years earlier.[2] I found that the little story somehow *fitted,* without knowing why. When I read you, I became aware of the reason.

The Goethe novel has had a surprising success in this country, although the translation, for all its merits, woefully corrupts it, in my opinion, necessarily eliminating all the small pleasures and subtleties of the language. But even so, it seems to succeed. The lack of the original version remains, nonetheless, hard to bear.[3] If the money were somehow available, it would be essential to establish here an international library of original editions in German, French, Italian, Spanish, Czech, and certainly Hungarian too.

Our summer in California, where the climate actually approaches the paradisical, was as good as it could be under the prevailing conditions. It took great efforts to save those who were imperiled in France. We were able to bring many over with the help of a committee founded especially for the purpose. My brother and our second son too are now fortunately with us. But this work continues, and I have not given up hope of arranging a position for you somewhere.

Yours sincerely,
Thomas Mann

1. *Das Ägäische Fest* first appeared in Albae Vigiliae, O.S. XI (Amsterdam, 1941); then in *Spiegelungen Goethes in unserer Zeit* (Wiesbaden, 1949); and separately in a third, augmented edition (Wiesbaden, 1950) (*HSF,* pp. 116–149).

[2.] See *Joseph and His Brothers,* pp. 867 ff. (*GW,* V, 1315 ff.).

[3.] The German edition of *The Beloved Returns* appeared in Stockholm in 1939 in a small printing which could still be distributed to certain countries, notably Sweden and Switzerland. Presumably few copies reached the United States at the time. See Thomas Mann, *Briefwechsel mit seinem Verleger Gottfried Bermann Fischer, 1932–1955* (Frankfort on the Main, 1973), pp. 252–257.

Kerényi to Mann

Budapest, November 15, 1940
XII. Zalai-ut 5/c

Dear Herr Professor!

To receive confirmation from a Goethe expert, and such a one as yourself, was in this instance more important than ever for me. You ask who first stated the idea that the marriage of Homunculus and Galatea is the preparation—I would say, the condition—for the Helen act. I can only speak of my own experience. During a whole semester I lectured here at the university on sea divinities and the Aegean scene [in the "Classical

Walpurgis Night" of *Faust,* Part II] was one of my sources, in fact a principal source. I was forced to interpret it thoroughly. It was then that I had the thought that Helen was reborn from *that* marriage. That was over a year ago. This spring, during my last trip, the last possible, to Italy, I read your Goethe novel and found support for my view in the 7th chapter. Only afterward, as I set down my interpretation of the scene this summer, did I look at the secondary sources and find the essay by Hertz in the *Germanisch-Romanische Monatsschrift*[1] on the conclusion of the "Classical Walpurgis Night," which makes a similar point on the basis of Goethe's scientific thought. Hertz's thesis is cited in my essay [*Das Ägäische Fest*], p. 20, though I consider its wholly unmystical approach inadequate.

But my experience with your Goethe novel was this: my head spun when I realized, at the very beginning of the 7th chapter, just *what* you had undertaken. And it continued to spin as I saw the achievement, as I began to realize how far intuitive apprehension could go. It is a step beyond Proust, a descent to the deep creative source which is Goethe, or rather, which Goethe too once was—and this signifies an original "mythological" achievement, in the sense that I understand mythology.

It was only when I resumed work on the Aegean scene this summer that I understood clearly the contrast between the "mysticism" of antiquity and that of the Orient and Christianity. My "Urkind" ["Primordial Child"] and *Das göttliche Mädchen* ["The Divine Maiden"], which appeared in my Albae Vigiliae series with a commentary by C. G. Jung, the Zurich psychologist, were preparatory stages for this.[2] All I have said about the similarity that exists between Goethe's mode of creation and the processes of mythology as revealed by recent research derives from the conclusions of those two studies and another on the labyrinth that was also written this summer.[3] In *Das göttliche Mädchen* I discuss the identity of mother and daughter, Demeter and Persephone, at length. I have sent the first version of that, entitled "Kore," to my friend Prof. Tolnay in Princeton. He would be the right person there to collect works originally written in Hungarian. This essay, however, like *Das Ägäische Fest,* was written in German.

My further plan, now that my *Religione antica* is to appear in German,[4] would be to write a basic, new work on the mysticism of antiquity. My studies of mythology point to that very subject, if only external circumstances do not stand in the way. The possibilities were there as long as I could use the libraries in Rome a few times each year. Now these dwindle. [. . .]

My family has also been enlarged—my daughter Lucia Magdalena Nike was born in June on the day that I wrote the introduction about the new "science of mythology" to my "Urkind," now entitled *Das göttliche Kind.* Other changes have come too. The path to a professorship in Budapest is more than ever blocked to me.[5] The Faculty of Philosophy in Pécs, where I have held a chair in classical philology up to now, has been dissolved, and I have to go to the provincial town of Szeged to lecture to 20 students. Since travel has become extremely difficult, I lack the necessary books—not to mention other conditions essential for fruitful intellectual activity.

With best greetings, from my wife too,

Ever your devoted,
Karl Kerényi

1. 7 (1915–1919), 281–300.

2. *Das göttliche Kind* appeared as O.S. VI–VII (Amsterdam and Leipzig, 1940), and *Das göttliche Mädchen* as O.S. VIII–IX (Amsterdam and Leipzig, 1941). They were published together in C. G. Jung and C. Kerényi, *Einführung in das Wesen der Mythologie* (Amsterdam and Leipzig, 1941; augmented ed., Zurich, 1951). In *Essays on a Science of Mythology: The Myth of the Divine Child and the Mysteries of Eleusis,* trans. R. F. C. Hull, Bollingen Series, XXII (New York, 1949), the two essays by Kerényi are entitled "The Primordial Child in Primordial Times" and "Kore."

3. For a Hungarian *Festschrift*. This became the *Labyrinth-Studien,* Albae Vigiliae, O.S. XV (Amsterdam, 1941); 2d, augmented ed., Albae Vigiliae, N.S. X (Zurich, 1950) (*HSF,* pp. 226–273).

4. As *Die antike Religion*. See Introduction, note 18. (An Italian translation [Bologna, 1940] had appeared before the German edition.)

5. A reorganization of the Hungarian universities under political pressure came about at the time. Those professors who refused to conform were isolated in a kind of "reservation" at the University of Szeged. About this, see my piece "Die ungarische Wendung," *Neue Schweizer Rundschau,* N.S. 12 (1945), 585 ff.

Mann to Kerényi

Princeton, February 18, 1941

Dear Herr Professor,

That you and Jung could find a common ground, mythology linked to psychology, is a most remarkable, propitious, and, in the present intellectual climate, highly characteristic achievement. *Das göttliche Kind* has indeed reached me.[1] It is an extremely interesting book—no wonder that something so wonderfully interesting results when two initiates of such stature join forces. It would amuse you to see how profusely marked and underlined the pages of my copy are. For my part, I have been delighted to see with what zeal and excitement I could still read when in my true element—and what should that be these days if not myth plus psychology. I have long been a passionate adherent of this combination, for actually psychology is the means whereby myth may be wrested from the hands of the Fascist obscurantists to be "transmuted" for humane ends.[2] For me this combination represents no less than the world of the future, a human community that is blessed by a spirit from above and "out of the depths that lie below."[3]

You see how important to me is the principle that lies behind your joint work, not to mention its specific content, which

[100]

is rich and fascinating, and which, incidentally, has confirmed for me, through many details, that there is a very correct instinct behind my own unscholarly mythological musings. I could not help being pleased to note that the psychopompos is characterized as essentially a child divinity: I thought of Tadzio in *Death in Venice*. And the absence of a "unity of the individual" in primitive thought of which Jung speaks is something that I have treated quite on my own as a humoristic element in *The Tales of Jacob* (Eliezer).[4] These are two examples. The mythological figure who of necessity attracts me more and more these days is the moon-oriented Hermes, about whom I have read excellent things in this book. He has already been a haunting presence here and there in the Joseph books; but in the last volume, where the hero is shown as a statesman and businessman of sovereign cunning, this figure changes more and more from the original Tammus-Adonis role to that of a Hermes. His actions and transactions cannot be well rendered in moral and aesthetic terms except in the spirit of a divine rogue's tale.

I have recently sent off a small book to you, *The Transposed Heads* [1940], an Indian legend and nothing more than a metaphysical jest. But perhaps you will enjoy it. Since your package reached me, let me hope that mine will be equally fortunate.

Let us hope that the connection with Europe does not break off completely! The very possibility that this may happen reinforces my wish that you might join the transatlantic European community here, in this country which will, after all, *nolens volens* [willy-nilly], surely assume the leadership of the world. "Exile" has become something wholly different than in the past; it is no longer a condition of waiting oriented to a homecoming but a foretaste of a dissolution of nations and a unification of the world. A professorship in mythology should be established here, and in fact for you; I say so constantly. But they seem not to have a proper understanding here of the new status of this field as you represent it.

With my warmest wishes and greetings,

Yours,

Thomas Mann

1. See Kerényi to Mann, November 15, 1940, note 2.

[2.] In referring to "Fascist obscurantists" who had debased the concept of myth, Mann had in mind men like Alfred Rosenberg, whose *Der Mythus des 20. Jahrhunderts* (1930) was one of the most widely read tracts on the Nazi racial "myths." In his 1942 lecture on the Joseph novels, Mann was to write, "The word 'myth' is in bad repute at this time—one has only to think of the title that the 'philosopher' of German Fascism, Hitler's teacher Rosenberg, gave his infamous tract" (*GW,* XI, 658).

In this and the following letter Mann adopts the neologism *umfunktionieren* (which we translate "transmute") from Ernst Bloch, who in letters to Mann had cited *Joseph and His Brothers* as an outstanding example of the "Umfunktionierung des Mythos," in the sense in which Bloch develops the notion in chapter xv of *Das Prinzip Hoffnung* (Frankfort on the Main, 1959). (Manfred Dierks's 1967 Freiburg dissertation, "Studien zu Mythos und Psychologie bei Thomas Mann," pp. 356 f., establishes this link to Bloch.) Mann cites Bloch in this connection in other letters, in *Briefe, 1937–1947,* ed. Erika Mann (Frankfort on the Main, 1963), pp. 262, 579.

3. From Joseph's response to Amenhotep in Volume IV of the novel *Joseph and His Brothers,* p. 937 (*GW,* V, 1422).

[4.] *Joseph and His Brothers,* pp. 279 ff. (*GW,* IV, 419 ff.).

Mann to Kerényi

Pacific Palisades, California, September 7, 1941

Dear Herr Professor,

Let me assure you that *Das göttliche Mädchen*[1] has in fact reached me, and that this exceptionally interesting work has given me the greatest pleasure and instruction. You will find traces of this one day in the chapter of the last Joseph volume

[*Joseph the Provider*] that deals with the marriage of Joseph, elevated to lordship, with the girl Asenath of On, on which I am just working. Since virginity encounters virginity here, I felt justified in making a kind of mystery rite of it in which I boldly, or if you will shamelessly, use something of Demeter-Eleusinia. This is not so un-Egyptian, since the wandering, searching mother is after all also at home on the Nile, and the relationship of Demeter and Isis is obvious, although in the latter case there is a murdered *son*. At any rate, in this final volume the various mythologies—Jewish, Egyptian, Greek—mix so freely that one license more or less will make no difference.

The kind of joint effort that has developed between us over the years, although at a distance and imperceptible to the uninitiated, is as legitimate as your highly fruitful and fortunate scholarly collaboration with Jung. This cooperative labor of mythology and psychology is a most gratifying phenomenon! It is essential that myth be taken away from intellectual Fascism and transmuted for humane ends. I have for a long time done nothing else.

I am grateful that you have not deprived me of the Kore book! It offers imposing testimony to your growth as a scholar.

We have already lived in California four months and intend to remain here. Seven Palms House, on its hill, already has a roof and will be ready for occupancy in the late fall. I fear that the longing for Europe will have almost been put to sleep by the time your desperate part of the world becomes accessible again. But for me a letter that has just come from my former publisher in Budapest represents a curiously exhilarating symptom—a letter in which he says that he considers the connection with me only "temporarily" suspended. So now, they have begun to send out signals.

Cordially,
T. M.

1. See Kerényi to Mann, November 15, 1940, note 2.

Kerényi to Mann

Dear, honored Herr Professor,

I can hardly believe that I can resume a "prewar" custom today: to write to you before the end of the old year. But we have heard that contact by post with the United States has just become possible again, so I hope that this letter will reach you. Just a year ago I tried to forward to you two pieces of mine—*Hermes der Seelenführer*, a reprint from the *Eranos-Jahrbuch* of 1942, and my *Labyrinth-Studien*—along with a short account of what had befallen me. All this, unfortunately, without success. The letter was not sent on to you, although, I have been told, its personal message was communicated to you. Thus I assume that you know that I, together with my wife and two small daughters, was able to reach Switzerland safely a year before the outbreak of the barbarities in Hungary, both the earlier and the more recent. The two older daughters remained in Hungary. One of them had already been denounced for her openness of speech during the Horthy phase of the German terror in Hungary and transported to Auschwitz; and since November we have not heard anything of the other one either.[1] A true Christmas joy is the rescue of my friend the psychologist Dr. [Leopold] Szondi of Budapest, who made his way to Switzerland along with 1300 other Jewish companions in vicissitude.

The arrival of this important researcher in depth psychology, inventor of a new, exact method of testing; the old collaboration with Prof. Jung continuing along parallel lines but without in the least deflecting me from my own path; and the possibilities of publication in Switzerland (the *Hermes* appeared as the first issue of a new series of my Albae Vigiliae in the Rhein-Verlag, and Rascher will put out a pamphlet[2] and a small book[3] of mine, which you will receive upon publication)—all these lead me to hope that the salutary task of the humanist mythologist which you called "the transmutation of myth for humane ends" may be fulfilled even under wholly altered circumstances. When my professorship in Hungary was terminated, effectively if not legally, the University of Basel gave me a visiting post teaching Hungarian. And although I do not want to disdain either the honor accorded me or the good fortune that allows me to keep alive the intellectual heritage of my native land, I still cannot ignore the negative side of the situation. I do not want to compare myself with such great men as Bachofen and Nietzsche, who were also given appointments by the University of Basel in fields uncongenial to them: Bachofen in law and Nietzsche only as a philologist, although the former at first nurtured an unfulfilled longing for archaeology and the other sought the professorship of philosophy. It is conceivable that both of them were forced to develop their particular "venom" precisely in consequence of such partial solutions . . . In any case, charlatanism and intellectual mediocrity found it easier to attach themselves to great men who did not enjoy academic recognition, and this undoubtedly turned out to be unhealthy.

In my case the issue involves my conscious separation from philology in Wilamowitz' sense. Not that I have separated myself from its insights—one does not give up the knowledge acquired in youth, and in my case it often serves me now in place of a library (my own was left in Hungary). No, that separation was rather a disengagement from what I found alien from the start, a soil in which the pursuit of classical studies and research by almost the whole world had been forcibly rooted ever since 1870: the soil of Prussia. You will be astonished to see after the war how many philologists, even after emigration and in countries that have remained free, will continue to stand unswervingly on the old, essentially unfree foundations! My separation, the liberation from that alien soil and the fruitful discovery of my own intellectual roots—significantly enough, considered forbidden and revolutionary even by my earlier Hungarian colleagues—provided the initial occasion for our correspondence. That was my lecture on Apollo, and even the fact that I sent it to you at the time, exactly eleven years ago, was an act of apostasy . . .

Your letters have been saved and are here now. I have many of my own in draft. (Of the important ones, perhaps only my letter about *The Beloved Returns* is missing [November 15, 1940]). The whole correspondence, in a process of organic growth, has become a small book, and for me personally an unintentional testimony of my true intellectual bases. And now as it stands, without forethought or plan, it is in fact a program. For, considering not only its objective scholarly importance and its cultural worth as a work of formulation and documentation, I as a scholar can still subscribe only to this intellectual program. For this reason I would have liked to initiate the new series of Albae Vigiliae that has originated here in this free soil (just as the original plan for these white nights of humanism originated in the then still free Norway) with the publication of our correspondence. Yet the Hermes book was already finished in 1942, and I felt compelled to publish it for reasons related to my situation after breaking "official" connections with Hungary. I did not want to publish the letters without your agreement, though they contain nothing personal. (I have, anyway, omitted purely ephemeral matter without intellectual or historical interest.) Thus I had no choice but to reserve the correspondence for the second number of my series and to take the first opportunity to request your consent.

I do so now, while sending you a copy of the book as I plan it. (The letter about *The Beloved Returns* should be added if you possess it and can send me the original or a copy.) I would of course be happy if you wished to add a preface to my introduction. At this distance I did not dare to count on it. I trust the dedication will meet with your approval.[4] In writing it, I thought specifically of certain young men and above all of my daughter Grazia, who—like the older one Katharina, in fact —was a student of classical philology and just at work on the Hungarian version of my *Apollo* when the Gestapo arrested her. The date of my introduction [see Introduction, p. 25, above] is that of her 19th birthday [September 8, 1944].

You will see from the introduction that I was just reading *The Tables of the Law* [1944] at the time, and I am truly delighted that Swiss critics are gradually returning to a note of true enthusiasm for your work. I had written about the last volume of *Joseph*, although only briefly, in that letter that did not reach you, touching on its radically progressive elements. Now, looking back from the Moses story [*The Tables of the Law*], I see how that volume already prepared for it. Once I can feel again that I am in correspondence with you, that my words do not fade away short of their goal—"goal" in the sense of the Greek *telos*, as fulfillment—then I shall perhaps be able to go into more detail about that. I do not know at the moment, in fact, whether you are already in a position to reply to this letter. But since the projected publication will be of both scholarly and humanistic interest, since it may be of importance not only in my special field but in the present cultural situation as a whole, I would hope to get word of your agreement somehow, at least on this point. A simple "yes" would suffice. If a proper letter comes once again, that will be a mythological event—precisely because it is so fundamentally normal and human, as mythology is in its deepest sense.

[107]

With the best greetings, wishes, and hopes for the year '45,
Ever your devoted
Karl Kerényi

[1.] The "Horthy phase" or "earlier" barbarities in Hungary came between March and July 1944, when Miklós Horthy (1868–1957), the regent, was in effect forced to surrender control of the government to the Germans. A roundup and deportation of Jews as well as many liberals and Legitimists was the consequence. The later phase came after October 15, when an attempt by Horthy to surrender to the Russians collapsed and a renewed wave of deportations took place.

Both of the daughters discussed here survived the war, as the translator has learned from one of them, Dr. Caterina (Katharina) Kerényi, now residing in San Diego, California. See Kerényi to Mann, February 26, 1946.

2. *Bachofen und die Zukunft des Humanismus, mit einem Intermezzo über Nietzsche und Ariadne* (Zurich, 1945).

3. *Töchter der Sonne: Betrachtungen über griechische Gottheiten* (Zurich, 1944).

4. It reads, "To the young intellectuals who suffered in the war." (Kerényi amplified the dedication slightly for the complete edition of the correspondence.)

Kerényi to Mann

Zurich, February 3, 1945
Hotel Sonnenberg

Dear Herr Professor Mann,

Your telegram,[1] the first meaningful sign that our desperate corner of the world (as you called it in your farewell letter in 1941) has again become accessible, arrived today just as the time has become ripe for the publication of our correspondence. I could not better characterize the present intellectual confusion in humanistic studies than by enclosing a letter I recently felt compelled to write.[2]

[108]

My dear Colleague!

The morning paper brought me a singular surprise: a droll memorial (and God knows, I love such jests of fate) of our long-standing, silent relationship. Indeed, I do not know anymore how many years I have seen you, when from time to time I pop into the Zentralbibliothek, invariably in the same corner of the reading room, entrenched behind philological reference works. You sat there after your bitter emigation, chased from your native Austria, while I used to come from Hungary and then later from Tessin, which finally became my home in exile. I leaf through one or another of those works much more anxiously than you, like one who is forced to work from memory and wants to reassure himself that everything he has accumulated in Greece and Italy, from the classical authors ravenously devoured in youth and from the researches of maturer years, is real, is there, and not a dream. Oh, all those dreams of philologians that are brought together and fulfilled in this most unexpected of places—how they transfigure everything in this reading room!

In our relationship that had thus been established a change occurred recently. I learned through a sympathetic librarian that you wished to know where a rather delicate detail about the love relation of Zeus and Hera could be found, a passage in a Greek author to which I allude in my *Töchter der Sonne*.[3] Thus I was forced to break our silence and come to your aid and at the same time, involuntarily, to come to the aid of that lengthy discussion of my little book which appears in today's paper, a discussion in which you inform me that I neither adduce all the available evidence from Greek sources nor show any wish for such completeness. My very dear colleague, isn't absolute completeness available to you there, behind your back, in the handbooks and encyclopedias of classical studies? And didn't we both search there for that delicate passage—in vain? Only weeks afterward could I indicate the source to you. Isn't it clear that the completeness of the best lexicons is only relative and that we, who have grown gray and melancholy amidst the incompleteness of the assembled ruins of antiquity, must resign ourselves and must learn

[109]

to limit our selection to those few and most essential bits of data that we have the power to revivify . . .

And here I would like to direct your attention to something more general, for I am not writing this letter to amuse myself concerning our mutual limitations. Our scholarly discipline has experienced periods that are alternately extensive and intensive. It is the same in our individual research activity. So long as we gather and search, we act extensively; our ideal is "completeness," the unattainable. As soon as we really "find" something, we are inwardly forced to become intensive. And since the extensive methods are easily learned, we must invent the no less important intensive ones. Whoever does not possess the same degree of intensity will hardly notice how demanding such a method can be, for he will himself usually be unreceptive to the aim of this method. This must have happened to you when you took exception to a play of words I had allowed myself in a German book only for purposes of elucidation, calling it an example of my "method." You did not notice that though the words are German, the matter is Greek: it appears in Aeschylus, clear and unequivocal, in the verses that I cite.

Indeed, you present me with an altogether universal problem. How is it that well-trained philologians are capable of not noticing what stands in the texts? There is also a normal "not noticing." As a matter of fact, the very possibility of continuing our scholarly work depends in part upon this. You certainly know Jacob Burckhardt's words: "Everyone must reread the books that have already been repeatedly ransacked, since they show a particular countenance to each reader and to each epoch, and also to each period in the life of an individual. It may be that a fact of indubitable importance is to be found in Thucydides, for example, which someone will notice only after a hundred years."[4] This is all the more true of the mythological texts. But there are certain limits too, and in invoking the famous Wilamowitz, the last great dictator of philological studies, as a mighty shield against my almost playful book of the moment, you forestall any possible solution of the problem. To kill intensity by means of extension, to divert attention from the meaning of a text by piling up dead, forgotten data—in this Wilamowitz was the great master.

It seems to you, of course, that his method, the so-called method of historical philology, draws scrupulously on "the real facts," since it utilizes only transmitted sources. On this point I could not help but be saddened by reading your exposition, for the surrender of the healthy skepticism of the great, truly historical minds of the nineteenth century signifies the end of the scientific investigation of history itself. To believe that speculation—yes, mysticism—is always on the other side testifies to a wholly unhistorical self-assurance. Allow me to reveal something to you. There is a kind of relationship that develops from living with the heritage and the monuments of antiquity over many decades that does not depend on speculation; but then, "when a man has devoted himself to this and come to feel at home in it, there suddenly arises, as if kindled by a jumping spark, something like a fire in the soul, and from then on it continues to feed itself."[5] These words are by Plato, whom even Wilamowitz credited with a scientific spirit. It is precisely the purely historically oriented philology that must continually utilize speculation. Since it has in advance rejected any inherent meaning in mythologems, it is forced on occasion to *speculate* on the origin of such imaginings. There is just no other way, for this origin itself is not transmissible, not knowable. The preoccupation with what is not knowable consumed the strength of whole generations of scholars who were reared in the merely historical school; it prevented them from seeing what is vital and meaningful in the thought of antiquity and from grasping its fundamental and unique qualities.

Had you never noticed how Wilamowitz himself remains trapped within the narrow confines of his domineering, Prussian self-assurance without even recognizing the possibility of a fundamentally different world view, such as the Greek? When, in *Der Glaube der Hellenen,* he describes the origin of animal-shaped divinities—in this case of Pan—what he writes sounds so perfectly natural, although it is the purest speculation: "When a man encounters a bear or a hind or a wild he-goat in the wilderness, it may often enough be just the animal, but in a particular instance what he sees becomes uncanny: this was no bear, no hind; it was a god. Who it was is not deduced from the nature of the animal; rather, the man had already brought with him a faith in a specific god and now he perceives him in this embodiment; the god is after all free to choose how he wishes to show himself." Please note how precisely Wilamowitz is informed about matters regarding which we have no evidence, and could not have any—what the man brought with him, what the god was free to do. But there is still proof to come, and from a witness of indisputable authority: "*I myself* experienced an epiphany of him," writes Wilamowitz about Pan, "as I rode through a narrow pass in Arcadia and a noble he-goat suddenly appeared in the branches of a tree over my head . . . "[6] Is this what is meant by drawing scrupulously on "the real facts, the transmitted sources"? I can see only two "real facts" here: the he-goat and the professor from Berlin.

But we are dealing today with something more serious than the unintentional humor of this kind of authoritarian scholarship. You will, dear colleague, probably soon make your way home again, for which you have my very best wishes. I can also recommend some light reading for the journey, an amusing little book about classical philology by a fellow Hungarian, Ludwig [Lajos] Hatvany, a book with the memorable title *Die Wissenschaft des nicht Wissenswerten* [Leipzig, 1908; "Scholarship of What Is Not Worth Knowing"]. It was not difficult for him after his period of study in Berlin about 1906 to reveal the human insufficiency of that merely historical method of philology which subsequently became more inclusive but also more presumptuous rather than humane. But in this connection you should also read Wilamowitz' own memoirs. One views them today with different eyes than before the world-shaking events that have occurred since 1938. You will note in them, perhaps, how with the aid of the high Prussian official [Friedrich] Althoff a kind of scholarly one-party system was created in the universities for making appointments in classical philology, a system whose superiority you unintentionally proclaim to today's uninitiated newspaper readers. Please consider before returning to your sphere of activity whether you wish to revive and maintain that system in the humanistic studies of your native land.

This is what I wrote, but, I very much fear, in vain. For the power of early training is great. I shall probably not even send off this letter to a particular individual. The issue today does not involve individuals but an awareness that the intellectual situation now requires free inquiry above everything else. I have myself seen in what ungodly contradictions the staunch defenders of the Wilamowitz school became entangled—not to mention much worse—when faced by this challenge, contradictions very different from those of this critic, whom I could well have invented as a typical example. Let my words to him remain in our correspondence as a general warning that things are now very different, and especially that the responsibility is much greater than in the times before Bachofen and Nietzsche. That great Basel figure [Nietzsche] could still draw back mockingly when the historical school refused to acknowledge his authority in classical scholarship. And you will recall Nietzsche's symbolic words about his episode with Wilamowitz: "As I lay asleep, a sheep nibbled at the ivy wreath that lay on my head—nibbled and at the same time said, 'Zarathustra is a scholar no more.' "[7]

The days for Zarathustra games are past. No one can any longer afford the leisure of slumbering in this fashion, least of all the humanist for whom a new era of awakening and alertness has come, perhaps a clearer and keener time than ever before. He must, more steadfastly than ever, defend the investigation of antiquity against becoming a scholarship of what is not worth knowing—indeed, of what is not knowable—and thus a violation of free intellect and the suicide of humanism. I am grateful that I can say these things now, as we resume our correspondence, and want to inform you also of another event, one that fills me with happy prospects: it is an event in our own family mythology—the birth of a son in the free Alpine air of this country.

Most devoted greetings from all of us!

Sincerely yours,
Karl Kerényi

1. From Santa Monica, California, January 31: "Delighted about renewal of contact no objection to publication sending missing letter warmest regards. Thomas Mann" (in English in the German edition).

[2.] This letter was prompted by a review of Kerényi's *Töchter der Sonne* by Franz Stoessl, an Austrian classicist, which appeared in the *Neue Zürcher Zeitung* of February 3, 1945. The article, entitled "Griechische Gottheiten," is an attack on Kerényi's scholarly method, which is contrasted to that of Ulrich Wilamowitz-Moellendorff. In Wilamowitz' interpretation of Greek religion, Stoessl argues, every mythologem regarding Greek divinities is carefully identified in terms of its local and temporal provenance, whereas Kerényi's practice is to combine uncritically examples from various periods of antiquity and even from postclassical sources. Stoessl further condemns Kerényi for not providing a comprehensive survey of the available sources from antiquity for the issues he deals with. "Such methods," he concludes, "bring forth a network of personal and subjective speculations but no objective, scholarly conclusions." The response by Kerényi was published in the newspaper *Weltwoche* on February 16, 1945. (Dr. Manfred Dierks kindly provided information on these sources.)

[3.] See Kerényi to Mann, December 21, 1944, note 3.

[4.] *Weltgeschichtliche Betrachtungen,* in *Gesammelte Werke* (Basel, 1956), p. 15.

[5.] Plato, Letter VII, 341 c–d (translation by Dr. Barbara K. Gold).

[6.] Ulrich von Wilamowitz-Moellendorff, *Der Glaube der Hellenen* (3d ed.; Basel-Stuttgart, 1959), I, 151.

[7.] *Thus Spake Zarathustra,* Part II: "Concerning the Scholars," in *Werke,* ed. K. Schlechta (Munich, 1955), II, 380.

PART II (1945–1955)

Humanism—Painful Destiny

Mann to Kerényi

Pacif. Palisades, Calif.
1550 San Remo Drive
[February 7, 1945][1]

Dear Herr Professor,

You already know from my telegram how delighted I was to make contact with you again and to have a token that you find yourself on free soil, able to resume the free life of the intellect. The news you write has in some measure the quality of the horror of the times—I am thinking of your older daughter and consider that there is little consolation in the fact that you share the hideous disintegration of your family with millions of others on that most unfortunate of continents. Is it possible that you have had news of the missing ones since you last wrote me? How happy I would be for you! If not—still there is a chance when the clouds have lifted, the waters drained off.

Of course, I knew that you had gotten to Switzerland. The question was whether you would be allowed to stay there—and this is now happily resolved. That small country has, on the whole, proved true and good and shown its adherence to its humanitarian tradition. You know, of course, that your writings, especially the *Labyrinth-Studien*,[2] have reached me and been warmly received; Joseph's marriage and the impudent montage that I managed there will have given you a veritably humoristic proof of that. Of course, the snail-patterned torchlight dance in that chapter is hardly in the strict, ancient Egyptian style.[3]

[117]

And now about the correspondence—what objection could I have to its publication? It gives the impression of a friendly, lively exchange and may indeed, as you think, have some documentary value. But it is much more your book than mine, and any introductory words by me would be wholly superfluous. I enclose a careful copy of the missing letter, with the passage about *The Beloved Returns*.

Our life here, meanwhile, has taken its course through work and diversion, sickness and health, quite free of any privation worth mentioning (in this inexhaustible country all "shortenings"[4] partake of sport or racketeering). Following the interlude of the Moses story [*The Tables of the Law*], and in spite of many smaller literary obligations that the war effort brings with it, I have been working on my Faust novel [*Doctor Faustus*]—the fictional biography, written by a friend, of a German, a very German musician (composer) who shares the fate of Nietzsche and Hugo Wolf.[5]

I didn't know that *The Tables of the Law* was already available in Switzerland. There is a touch of Voltaire in that tale, don't you think, that had not yet found its way into the Joseph work. If only I could read the Swiss reviews!

Keep well! I feel that there will be a reunion.

Yours,

Thomas Mann

[1.] Date of postmark.

[2.] See Kerényi to Mann, November 15, 1940, note 3.

[3.] Cf. *Joseph and His Brothers,* pp. 1005 f. (*GW,* V, 1523 f.).

[4.] This word is in English in the original edition.

[5.] Wolf (1860–1903), Austrian composer best known for his *Lieder,* became insane in the last years of his life. Cf. Kerényi to Mann, August 13, 1934, note 3.

Kerényi to Mann

Ascona, March 15, 1945
(the day your letter of February 7, 1945, arrived)
Dear, honored Herr Professor,

To the letter I wrote with great, joyful excitement on the day your telegram arrived, I must add a postscript:

I see now that in those sentences about the alertness and steadfastness of the humanists there was perhaps too strong a note of confidence. The more I wish to be no more than an instrument of interpretation—as I indicated in the preface to our correspondence, which you have read—the greater seems to me the difficulty of realizing my goal of a free humanistic scholarship. At the beginning of my career, when I protested against the appropriation of philological studies for nationalistic ends that stripped them of both Hellenistic and humanist elements, I invoked Spitteler's phrase "Mein Herz heisst Dennoch."[1] Now I am compelled to add to these words of Spitteler's Herakles the insight of the Hungarian poet [Endre] Ady [1877–1919], whose words ("A muszáj-Herkules") I can best translate into French: one still remains a "Herakles" in that sense, but a "Hercule malgré lui" [in spite of himself]. You will, I am sure, understand my use of the word "humanist" in this connection. I utilize it, not arbitrarily, but with the historical significance I once gave it in that talk we had in the Schiedhaldenstrasse in Küsnacht, where I have often since made a pilgrimage: to designate a destined protector and preserver—a protector and preserver also *malgré lui*—of the shared, transmitted treasures of European man, an inheritance that must be salvaged from an old world and passed on to a

[119]

new. And yet—how many other things one must also be today *malgré lui!* There is simply no helping it.

I had to add this so as not to appear before you as a battle-hungry hero, but as the prisoner of a calling which cannot be laid aside even if other possibilities—if, in fact, *nothing but* other possibilities—lie before him. Will they understand in the new Hungary that there may be some use for me even *just* as I am? Or will I soon be confronted with a vexing problem? It is not altogether easy to return to a peacetime mood, even if we disregard our worry about near ones who have not sent any word for months now, and in spite of the beauty of the spring-time we are experiencing here for the third time—lovelier than ever, this season, with the three children who have their milk and their warm beds, something so normal and yet so marvel-ous that it allows me to forget all my burdens. The third of the three blond angels, our first son, who is now seven weeks old, is called Dionys Karl Antoninus, and everyone thinks that I have endowed him with showy classical names so that his life will be marked from the start as that of a mythologist's son. Yet his name is not Dionysos but Denys, after my closest friend in Hungary, Dionys Kövendi, who dared to continue his cor-respondence with us longer than anyone else but now also be-longs to those who have been silenced. And the name Antoninus came to me, not from Antoninus Pius or Marcus Aurelius Antoninus, though I hold them both in high esteem, but from the guardian saint of a small village here in Tessin that I drive past so often, a village called Sant'Antonino, between Cade-nazzo and Giubiasco. The bearer of these names is marked as much by the simplest forms of the spirit as by the complicated ones of his father . . .

And since I am on the subject of complicated things, I must confess to you that I read *The Tables of the Law* after the last volume of the mythological novel with the same pleasure as the novel itself. You say that a touch of Voltaire has crept into this story of Moses. I already felt his presence in the last volume of the Joseph novel. It is precisely this that I found so extraordinary there: that you were able to combine, ever more explicitly and strongly, an affirmation of the mythological dimensions of our spiritual life with a stance that testified to the freedom of the intellect. In the introduction to our correspondence I spoke of the singular postmythological spirit of *The Tables of the Law* and meant by this "spirit" exactly what you associate with Voltaire. In antiquity this style was called "euhemeristic," after the "blasphemer" Euhemerus. The achievement of this "enlightener" (which is what I must call Euhemerus, since he was actually neither philosopher nor poet) was that in the Alexandrian period he transformed mythology into pseudo-historical fiction, the gods into mortals of a primal age, and, through this interpretation of the Greek revelation, established a following. This constituted the "postmythological" in antiquity, and it appears again, unexpectedly and yet "on schedule," in your story of Moses. Nietzsche's words could serve as a motto to both your Biblical tales, the *Joseph* and the Moses story: "Concerning great things one should speak greatly, that is to say, cynically."[2] But most people are not mature enough to grasp this and hardly notice how much "greater than great" the truly great theme of this story—namely, *the law* as a moral and human force—seems, precisely by virtue of the cynical presentation of the religious element. This is what shocks and overwhelms the reader.

I shall close here, since this letter has already been interrupted by an obligatory trip to Lugano and a restorative stay in Montagnola.

With warm greetings,

Yours,
K. K.

[1.] "My heart proclaims 'Nonetheless' "—Herakles' defiant words on his expulsion from Olympus at the conclusion of Carl Spitteler's verse epic *Olympischer Frühling,* in *Gesammelte Werke* (Zurich, 1945), II, 609.

[2.] *Werke,* III, 634. The aphorism is actually "Great things require that one either keep silent about them or speak greatly: greatly, that is to say, cynically and with innocence."

Mann to Kerényi

1550 San Remo Drive
Pacific Palisades, California
September 23, 1945

Dear Herr Professor,

On receiving the copies of your *Mythologie und Romandichtung*[1] yesterday—two unbound and one bound, with your cordial dedication—I realized with shame how long our correspondence has been in abeyance—and how much through my fault. I found your letter of mid-March again, which came to me on May 7, according to the local postmark. At the time, our voyage to the east was soon to come, before which I gave a lecture at the Library of Congress in Washington, "Germany and the Germans" (to appear in German in *Die Neue Rundschau,* which will resume publication on my birthday).[2] Then there was a lengthy stay in New York, into which we squeezed a country visit (to Lake Mohonk, in the picturesque approaches to the Adirondacks). Then yet another visit, this one to the Borgese family in Chicago (our youngest daughter). There too festivities—altogether a jubilee, and also a jubilant trip, with some impressive observances, of which the highpoint, in public terms, was the large banquet at the Waldorf-Astoria in New York given by the Secretary of the Interior. [Harold] Ickes, Justice [Felix] Frankfurter of the Supreme Court, the Spanish Consul [Juan] Negrin, and others spoke—it was something of a political affair. All these events were a strain, and yet I returned refreshed and cheered by many happy impressions of sympathy, of the "goodwill of our contemporaries," as Goethe says. Also, one feels exceptionally well in this climate after a change of air, which is to be recommended once a year.

But immediately upon my return there was pressing work. I had agreed to do the introduction to an edition of Dostoevsky's shorter novels for a New York publisher, having "by chance" taken a number of them along with me on the trip. One is used to such accidents. The piece came of itself. It became an improvisation about sickness and *life* and thereby, as usual, an offshoot of the little thing on which I am just engaged—for two years now, and it already runs to 500 pages, which, I declare in desperation and joy, make up a good two-thirds of the dear work. Its title: [*Doctor Faustus:*] *The Life of the German Composer Adrian Leverkühn as Told by a Friend* [1947]. The friend is a humanist who tremblingly recounts a gruesome, unhumanistic tale. For this Adrian shares the fate of Nietzsche, of Hugo Wolf, etc., and is veritably a son of hell. The pact with the devil is the main theme of the book, which covers the period from 1885 to the arrival of Hitler, but stands with one foot in the German sixteenth century. Will this be something for our classical philologian and mythologist? But a colleague of his writes it, warm of heart, and is infinitely devoted to the cold demon.

So there was this or that and always the jog and the compulsion of the endless addresses, obligations, and affairs; thus your letter and the often very stimulating friendship had to be laid aside, this friendship to which our mythological correspondence testifies in such a moving way for me. Yes, it was not without emotion that I read through all of them again yesterday—these fragments of two autobiographies communicatively intertwined. And there was satisfaction too. For all this really maintains a very nice, decent, humane level, and—let us say it

[123]

outright—represents a perfectly presentable, in these days an almost exemplary cultural attainment, in a world of the most shocking cultural void.

I was strangely affected to reread what I wrote you in 1941 [February 18] from Princeton about "exile" and to note the change in meaning that has come about since: the word no longer simply denotes a waiting period oriented toward a homecoming but already suggests a conception of the world that transcends national limits. That passage has assumed a relevance for me at this time that is nothing short of irritating. The dear Germans are giving me a hard time of it. I have been "called upon." I am expected to return! No sooner has judgment day broken over Germany than I am to throw back my citizenship to the United States, sell my house, leave my children and grandchildren, abandon my work, and hurry back to Germany in order to take my part in a state of misery against which I warned tirelessly for twelve long years. Something about this call seems less than just to me. But still more shameless is the attitude of those colleagues who, because they did not open their mouths, found themselves so well situated in 1933 that they did not have to leave home, and now they behave as if they had stuck it out in the fatherland through heroic loyalty, while I . . . Stay-at-home jackasses is what they are, bench warmers of misfortune, who have learned nothing and forgotten nothing, and I am debating inwardly whether I shouldn't tell them so.

We too have no intention of forgetting anything, but we have learned a thing or two; isn't that so?

"As ten years ago," I am still ever myself,

Yours,

Thomas Mann

[1.] The title should be *Romandichtung und Mythologie,* Albae Vigiliae, N.S. II, (Zurich, 1945), the first part of this correspondence, published separately.

[2.] "Deutschland und die Deutschen," *Die Neue Rundschau,* 56 (1945), 4–21 (*GW,* XI, 1126–1148).

Mann to Kerényi

1550 San Remo Drive
Pacific Palisades, California
December 3, 1945

Dear Professor Kerényi,

A marvelous package![1] All of it admirable testimony to your concentration, your enthusiasm, your productive powers! I am truly grateful for the excitement and stimulation that have come to me from these writings. It seems to me that you already enjoy a well-established and widely respected role in Swiss cultural life. Do you still think of returning to your native land, whose problematic situation you have analyzed in the *Neue Schweizer Rundschau* with great perspicacity and, understandably, not without an undertone of personal involvement? Soon you will be in a position to enlighten the Swiss regarding their own situation, for what country does not have its problematic side? In this colossal, victorious, and "powerful" nation here, the last refuge of bourgeois *complacency,*[2] the atmosphere is so charged that one wonders whether it can all continue for long without some serious eruption. Clearly, your residence in Switzerland and your use of the German language offer as good a basis as before—possibly even better—for disseminating your scholarly as well as your humanistic anthropological impulses to the world at large. Regarding this question of the language, which is after all not your mother tongue (though one easily forgets that in your case), I would urge vigilance and constant recourse to your poetic conscience, which you must certainly take into account in treating the sublime themes you deal with. "Wie nahe eine solche Frage in

[125]

der Zeit der 'Pariser Rechenschaft' lag, ebenso unmöglich erscheint sie . . ." This is not a logical construction in German. It would be correct simply as "So nahe . . . so unmöglich." Or one would have to say, "Wie nahe auch eine solche Frage etc. . . . sie erscheint unmöglich, sobald etc." This example is, understandably, not *altogether* isolated. Fussiness? Pedantry? I can only appeal, once more, to the great dignity of your subject matter.

As you see, in spite of the fascinating band with the golden, shimmering eyes (a wonderful idea!),[3] and in spite of the mystifying son of Maia,[4] that enticing divinity who calls forth ever renewed attempts at interpretation, I found myself most eagerly drawn to the Bachofen-Nietzsche piece, which at the moment belongs most directly in my own (magical or incantatory) sphere. For *verily,* as one used to say, *verily* is not[5] this perhaps impossible novel on which I have been struggling forward since May of 1943 in essence a Nietzschean novel and thus also slightly touched by the spirit of myth, although it takes place, not three thousand years ago, but during the time of our last war and actually deals with the character and fate of Germany? If only as a work of old age, it has a certain, though admittedly remote, similarity to [Hermann Hesse's] *The Glass Bead Game* [1943]. The figure of Nietzsche is more directly present in my novel than that of Bachofen, who is no longer so important for my work as in the period of *Joseph.* You understand perfectly, of course, to what a degree my passing remarks about Bachofen in the twenties were prompted by apprehensions of a political nature and concern over the biased way in which he was then treated and exploited.[6] He is, after all, in spite of his keen sense of what lies "below" (without which there could be no humanity), in no sense an obscurantist; in fact, his system of thought culminates in an affirmation of the religion of Zeus. The juncture at which this appeared and the manner of presentation seemed to me unpropitious in pedagogical terms, but as for myself, I never feared this mythologist from Basel and have studied him deeply—almost as much as Schopenhauer. Your essay brings up Bachofen's poetical conception of a swampy materiality, his symbolism of aquatic plants and swamp fauna, and in reading it I was reminded, not without a certain glee, of Potiphar's "exalted little parents" in the third Joseph book, those connubial siblings who endlessly shower one another with such terms of endearment as "dear mud-lark," "my swamp-beaver," "marsh marigold," "my good spoon-bill," "mole," and "barn owl"[7]—they know no bounds in thus demonstrating their archaic affinity to a prematriarchal "æon," parodying Bachofen all the while.

May everything continue well with you. My trip to Europe, at least for next spring as originally planned, appears ever more uncertain. First of all, *Doctor Faustus* will probably not be ready then, and secondly, I am constantly being warned in the most urgent terms about the unsettled conditions in Europe. It is simple enough to get over there, but then to travel on the Continent is evidently too adventurous and uncertain an undertaking for both my nerves and my stomach. On such occasions I have to confess that I feel more affinity with Erasmus than with Goethe.

Let us nonetheless hold fast to the hope for a reunion.

Yours,

Thomas Mann

1. It contained the *Neue Schweizer Rundschau,* with my piece "Die ungarische Wendung" (see Kerényi to Mann, November 15, 1940, note 5); the pamphlet on Bachofen, consisting of two essays that also originally appeared in the *Neue Schweizer Rundschau* (see Kerényi to Mann, December 21, 1944, note 2); *Töchter der Sonne* (see *ibid.,* note 3); and *Hermes der Seelenführer* (see Introduction, note 41).

[2.] This word is in English in the original.

3. In *Töchter der Sonne* this is related from the *Argonautica* of Apollonius of Rhodes.

4. Hermes.

[5.] Since the German here plays on the archaic style that Mann used extensively in *Doctor Faustus,* the "impossible novel" referred to, our translation can only be approximate. The original passage reads, "*Ist doch,* wie man früher im Deutschen gern sagte, *ist doch* der vielleicht unmögliche Roman . . . " (p. 123).

[6.] See Kerényi to Mann, March 1, 1934, note 1.

[7.] See *Joseph and His Brothers,* pp. 576 ff. (*GW,* IV, 858 ff.).

Kerényi to Mann

Ascona, December 19, 1945
Villa Sogno

My dear, honored Professor Mann,

Please forgive this rushed, typed letter. The rhythm of my life and work these days seems altogether subject to rush and pressure, prompted by external circumstances as well as inner tensions—all of which leave little chance for the epic flow of a long, relaxed letter. Time in the ordinary sense presses too. I see that I shall have to keep to the bare essentials if this letter is to be sent before Christmas and to reach you by the New Year. And I intend it to fulfill this pleasant secular-religious ritual and at the same time to respond to two of your letters.

You ask whether "The Life of the German Composer Adrian Leverkühn" [*Doctor Faustus*] will be something for the classical philologian and mythologist too? You have already seen my answer in the pamphlet about Bachofen with the Nietzsche intermezzo. You are right, of course, that the piece is linguistically very deficient. As is clear to me now, I wrote it in a period when I first realized that I was to be wholly dependent on German readers and auditors—this paradoxical necessity into which my good fortune had led me—and as a result my Hungarian nature reacted with exceptional intensity against a

language that had already become familiar to me through pro-
longed intellectual activity and the most intimate associations.
I reacted similarly in high school when I first had to learn
German after having already begun Latin. As long as I was
required to learn it, I always received poor grades in German.
It became mine only when it became a free adventure of the
mind. Initially, by mastering certain writers whom I had already come to cherish in translations—thus the first, the most
beloved author of my youth was the Swiss (is that a coincidence?) C. F. Meyer[1]—then finally, and seriously, by my own
writing activity.

Your work constituted one of the great acquisitions of my
youthful education, and now when you admonish me to be
strictly accountable to my poetic conscience in my own German writings, I can in no sense view this as pedantry, unless
it be of the Apollonian sort—the only kind I can endure. Indeed, how often have I looked for just such a sign, strict but
well-meaning, to guide me along the toilsome path I have
undertaken, a sign from a truly exalted, Apollonian seat of
learning! I have not gotten any from the masters of my own
discipline. Who then may be called masters of a humanistic
anthropology, in the sense in which you used the term, if not
intellects of a more independent, universal cast? You are also
right to stress the importance of one's location for disseminating the spirit of this kind of universal humanism; certainly
Switzerland is more suitable for that than Hungary, which is
for the present still relatively isolated from the West. I fear
only that you overestimate the role I could play in Switzerland.

I do not want to talk much about the fact that I have already suffered the typical fate of the conspicuous newcomer in
the village playground (and I could hardly remain inconspic-
uous with the Bachofen essay): to be splattered with mud by
the stupid children. [. . .] In psychologically oriented circles
there is a warm, sometimes almost unbelievable response to

mythology as I deal with it. But when I speak of humanism there is no response whatever, and the lack of understanding becomes still more marked when I speak of humanism as that state of progressive enlightenment that is part of the true progress of consciousness. Those few who do understand me remain isolated in the midst of the prevailing state of incoherence. It is seldom indeed that one of them achieves any direct, personal contact with me: the Swiss are well known for their reticence.

And I have sometimes had the impression that some of them, especially the younger ones, came to me, an outsider, more readily, with greater expectations, than they would have to one of their Swiss elders—but only the most dedicated intellects, the solitary spirits. Yes, you have guessed correctly: I would be capable of speaking of Switzerland's problems almost as competently as of Hungary's and with hardly any less emotional involvement. But I am, after all, only a stranger, and a conspicuous stranger, at an alien hearth—this image from C. F. Meyer's "Hochzeit des Mönchs," which I had read in my youth, came to me four years ago to symbolize my own situation as I found myself for the first time sitting at the hearth of a Swiss friend—and my gaze turns daily to the fatherland of *that* stranger whom Meyer depicts.[2] It is in a certain sense *also* my fatherland: the home of the gods of antiquity—and of humanism. What I envisage as my task, what I have perhaps already laid a foundation for in those smaller studies with which you are familiar, is something that will be both a theory of the divine and a theory of man, something that will proceed *beyond* Poliziano, but in no sense *with* Savonarola.[3] (How decisively you were already able to seize the issue *there,* in *Fiorenza,* that occupies you *now!* How happy I would be if we could one day, in conversation, meditate on this strand of your work that goes through Settembrini and our correspondence right to our friend Adrian Leverkühn!) A "comprehensive mythology" is still among my future plans, but also a "Life of Socrates," which would be a synopsis of the whole cultural history of Greece, the archaic as well as the classical. You will soon receive what constitutes the link between the *Hermes* and the "Socrates," between the figure who is able to live easily and the one who is able to die easily: my study of Prometheus, *the* fruit of all my labor during these years.[4]

I am convinced that I can also serve my fatherland only through my work, that activity which I pursue in an alien tongue become my own and which transmits something of the essence of Hungary to all men. The city where I could best pursue my work is Rome. Actually, a combination of Rome and Switzerland—not at all impossible in this age—would be the ideal solution. [. . .] I can't help but see something grotesque in the fact that our letters seem destined to come back to this theme even now, after the victory of the side of humanity. This undoubtedly reflects the condition of these times, when one would still like so much to bring about some change, to play some effective role, by means of the intellect.

This is my wish for the New Year: may you pursue your work in America untroubled by our concerns. Let the creation of works continue; there is probably no other way the artist and the scholar can have any effect on the world.

Most sincerely yours,
K. K.

[*Enclosed with this letter was the account of Grazia Kerényi sent from the Ravensbrück concentration camp.*][5]

[1.] C. F. Meyer (1825–1898), poet and fiction writer, is best known for his novellas.

[2.] Dante in Verona, exiled from Florence, is a character in the tale "Die Hochzeit des Mönchs" (1884).

[3.] Angelo Ambrogini Poliziano, fifteenth-century Florentine poet and humanist. Poliziano and Savonarola are characters in Mann's play *Fiorenza*. See Introduction, note 33.

[4.] See Mann to Kerényi, June 14, 1946, note 2.

[5.] See Kerényi to Mann, December 21, 1944, note 1; and Kerényi to Mann, February 26, 1946.

Mann to Kerényi

1550 San Remo Drive
Pacific Palisades, California
February 12, 1946

Dear Professor Kerényi,

My thanks to you, late and meager though they be, for your wonderful present of the *Geburt der Helena,* by which I mean, of course, the whole, rich garland full of erudition and deep thought collected under this title.[1] The book gives me the greatest pleasure, and will always continue to do so. There is something singularly elevating and purifying about such an immersion in a world of mythic consecration, human dignity, and the sacramental celebration of life. I use the word "sacramental" advisedly, for this proximity of the religious to the human, this passing of one into the other (most directly enunciated in the veritably theological essay about the spirit ["Der Geist"]), is perhaps what is most distinctive about this book, and perhaps too about the situation, the plight, of mankind in this age. For only if humanism moves toward the religious, something I can still view as possible without falling into an improbable dogmatism, can it acquire the binding force necessary to bring together the dispersed human race around a new source of authority. Without such an ideal gathering based on a sense of community and of piety the prospects would appear, as everyone feels, distinctly ominous, even hopeless, for that strange experiment "mankind."

Meager, I repeat, must be these words of thanks. You can not imagine how, in this childishly enthusiastic and well-meaning but at the same time naïvely exploitative country, one is constantly being solicited, dragged forth, and drained dry. And since the resumption of contact with Europe, my correspondence has doubled. "One's trials grow greater with the years," writes Goethe in a surprisingly Christian tone. The novel that I am pushing forward amid all the confusion and turmoil is devilishly difficult to realize. This is always the case with works of old age, and for good reason. Hesse's *The Glass Bead Game* is a lovely, grand, and moving example. Have you noticed that I appear in it as Magister Ludi Thomas von der Trave?

Soon I must interrupt my work in order to prepare for the yearly lecture tour to the East. Add to this a round trip to Europe, if one adopts the proposal of a certain agent in Brussels, for the man wants me to give lectures next May or June in London, Paris, Amsterdam, Brussels, and Zurich, at the least. A strenuous adventure, and almost everyone who thinks of my welfare warns me against it. The chief point, of course, would be the unavoidable visit to Germany—a most awkward matter, for I am again wholly at odds with this nation, which is offended by every word I utter. A terrible race! They must constantly find themselves offended and misunderstood, offended at all costs. And when one understands them all too well, they are all the more offended.

On the other hand, I say to myself that if I ever intend to appear there at all, I had better do it soon; otherwise the barriers will become insurmountable.

A true dilemma. What a shame that one is not a free private individual who can simply make a comfortable visit to Switzerland in order to see his friends again! But I have pretty well had to forfeit my private life on account of my audacity.

Yours sincerely,
Thomas Mann

1. *Die Geburt der Helena samt humanistischen Schriften aus den Jahren 1943–1945,* Albae Vigilae, N.S. III (Zurich, 1945).

Mann to Kerényi

1550 San Remo Drive
Pacific Palisades, California
February 17, 1946[1]

Dear Professor Kerényi,

I want to add these lines to the letter I wrote to thank you for the *Helena,* for not to have discussed at all the deeply moving document included in your letter of December 19 weighs on my mind. The account your daughter sent you of her experiences has touched me deeply, and I am most grateful to you for having conveyed it to me. What all these individuals have had to live through cries to heaven, and it is hardly conceivable that a young, delicate creature could withstand all she had to bear from an insane age and men devoid of any human stamp. To have the reunion with your daughter depend on the availability of "three buses" is yet another shameful and grotesque element of this affair. For heaven's sake, let the Red Cross think of the Hungarians, too, after helping the Czechs and the French, and somehow provide those three essential buses! I fervently hope that your daughter is with you as you read these lines.

Again, my warmest greetings.

Yours sincerely,
Thomas Mann

[1.] Typewritten.

[134]

Kerényi to Mann

Tegna, February 26, 1946
Tessin, Switzerland

Dear, honored Professor Mann,

Both your letters—the one of February 12 and the kind lines you wrote about Grazia's account of Ravensbrück—reached me here at this new station of my wandering existence. Yes, it is really unbelievable, a true miracle, but Grazia is finally home, in a Budapest plagued by winter and hunger. (From what I hear about the city, you would hardly recognize the castle. And whether Ludwig [Lajos] Hatvany's house, the Fortuna, still remains?) Grazia's account of her trip home is also a notable document: sick but with her own strength, and at the end—after her Jewish companions had received help from the synagogue in Bratislava—alone with six gypsies. I find something symbolic and tragic in the fate of those who are *not even* Jews. (Whose heart suffers for the gypsies, who were to be exterminated and were partly so in fact?—and yet one so often hears of the "musical nature" of the Germans!) . . . I sent you that first account of Grazia's with our correspondence in mind—that is, its dedication. You know that I thought primarily of her there, though not of her alone (the young scholar who intended "one day" to edit these letters died among the labor forces deported to the east)—and that the Introduction bears the date of Grazia's nineteenth birthday,[1] as homage to a victim from one who could not help her but wished to offer what he held most precious: the life and . . . yes, the *affliction* of the spirit where there was no bodily affliction.

It is remarkable that, in spite of the dedication, this motive for the publication of our letters (and of course there were others) was hardly noticed! *One* of the intentions was consciously pedagogical. A perceptive Swiss writer, Hans Nyffeler, otherwise unknown to me, saw this very much from your point of view: "Isn't there something exemplary about such a collaborative effort of the European mind, especially when it is achieved, as in this instance, with a dignity and respectful distancing that can hardly be found anymore?"—in the *Bund,* Monday supplement, August 6, 1945. (He also quotes the important part about "exile," a theme to which you recur in your most recent radio talk!) It may interest you further to see this excerpt from a letter (not addressed to me), which reflects the impression made by one of the first copies to reach Germany: "Of the books in the package, I read first the correspondence of K. with Thomas M. It excited me very much . . . At the same time, this correspondence between humanists, which reminds me of that of Erasmus and his friends, has a melancholy grace with which I can readily sympathize. It must be disheartening for them to write down so many subtleties and allusions which presuppose enormous learning and great maturity, knowing full well that the succeeding generation will already be unable to understand them."

I must confess to you that it is such evidence of "excitement" that repays me most for the publication. Yes, there were also those reasons for publishing that I have elucidated in the introduction, pertinent reasons, such as the proof of an archetypal correspondence between mythology and the form of the novel (the case of *cucullatus*).[2] Also pertinent would be the presentation of documents that reveal the very process of intellectual creation, demonstrating that it is not something that can be methodically practiced but must be experienced simply and directly, allowing full freedom to the unpredictable, the incalculable, what is called "spirit" . . . All reasons that need not be explicitly understood, so long as the effect I find so valuable is attained: namely, that this intimate play of the mind can still arouse excitement in some individuals, however few. A young friend and student in Rome, who returned from the German prison camps almost starved to death and is now an instructor at the university, read the letters "in a single night." Another, this one in Portugal, calls it "a book that one is compelled to read without interruption." Yet another, who reads German only with the aid of a dictionary (this one lives in Geneva and is not particularly close to me) read the book "in a winter night." Hesse found it "most stimulating"; a rabbinical scholar who fled from Germany to England wrote, though he did not know me, that he found it "intensely fascinating" . . .

Astonishing that this humanistic experience of ours, apparently so remote from real life, could arouse such fascination—Max Rychner in the *Tat* (June 16–17, 1945) characterized it as "an overwhelming instance, born of an auspicious constellation of discovery and recognition. Each is at work on a mythological tapestry and, viewing the other's evolving fabric with expert eyes, rejoices in discovering an unsuspected, fortunate confirmation of his own endeavors. Key words serve to awaken and elicit a response, and the act of expression is well-nigh a blessing."[3] It is satisfying and *consoling* to know that we could unintentionally awaken such fascination, even though our intended and specific aims are, for the time being at any rate, so little understood. The cause of humanism is not altogether lost as long as something like our "communicatively" but extemporaneously "intertwined" autobiographies (as you put it) are able to arouse such "excitement" [September 23, 1945]. And not lost, let me add, as long as one can still hear that *consummate* and deeply *human* language capable of expressing in full measure what has been thought and experienced, the language you used in the radio talk in order to make clear—and nothing in the world could be clearer to me—*why* you wish to be considered the homeless instrument of the spirit and not the

"German writer" as he is commonly [. . .] conceived. Yet such a supranational humanism—which, incidentally, coincides with Goethe's "German" nature—represents a spiritual commitment that I put alongside the greatest religious revelations of human history: "alongside," though not in the sense of an "either-or" but of a "this-as-well-as-that."

You are absolutely right to call for a movement of humanism toward the religious, for a gathering of minds in a spirit of piety and communal dedication. This sort of humanism we termed *religio Academici* in our correspondence (a term that is more than coincidentally related to the *Religio Medici* of an older English physician and humanist),[4] which, as you might expect, led some professional colleagues to object that it was "neither scholarship nor religion." And I very much fear that I shall soon be confronted with another either-or which will call in question my dream of a universally oriented humanistic career: *either* to return to my former academic post in the East and the kind of sterile involvement in party intrigues that you alluded to in your radio address (this would mean renouncing my plan to complete at least "Die Mythologie des Menschen," my "theory of the divine as a theory of man," utilizing the scholarly resources to be found here or in the true spiritual home of my project, Rome) *or* to renounce the citizenship of the country which still to a great extent continues to support me and my family—though partly by indirect means—and which I could then repay only in terms of the larger "world" —through my work and reputation . . . But how can one live for one's work when this *or* enters the picture? For a communal establishment of Jews and of Germans, of Swiss and of Mexicans exists. But of humanists or of gypsies?

How gladly I would describe the gypsy troop that surrounds my study here, in this small—perhaps the smallest—of Tessin villages, Tegna: a veritable little community of six, to which I would rather add my two grown daughters from Hungary than take those here into that misery. Should I then, in the name of this "humanism" that I talk about, lose and endanger yet more children in Hungary, rather than . . . ? Please forgive superfluous words, perhaps already too many. I thank you warmly for your two letters and greet you in the spirit of my long-standing devotion.

Yours sincerely,

K. K.

P.S. Tegna is at the entrance of the Centovalli Valley, near Locarno. I make a weekly trip to northern Switzerland. Travel conditions are still very comfortable in this country. Should you come here one day . . . I already long to make a trip north for *this* reason.

[*This letter did not reach Thomas Mann until a year later, as a copy.*]

[1.] September 8, 1944. See above, p. 25.

[2.] The hooded one. See Mann to Kerényi, February 20, 1934, note 6.

[3.] The review is incorporated in an essay on Kerényi, "Vom Umgang mit Göttern," in Max Rychner, *Zeitgenössische Literatur: Charakteristiken und Kritiken* (Zurich, 1947), pp. 115–130. The passage quoted is on p. 119.

4. See Kerényi to Mann, December 28, 1936, note 3. *Religio Medici,* by Sir Thomas Browne (1605–1682), was published in 1642.

Mann to Kerényi

Pacif. Palisades, Calif.

June 14, 1946

Dear Professor Kerényi,

Thank you for the entertaining newspaper clippings.[1] And very tardy thanks too for your *Prometheus.*[2] I can only hope that you had heard of my serious illness and operation; otherwise you must have considered me very discourteous and unreceptive. I wish you could see the many underlinings and exclamation points your work called forth. The Hermetic cynicism on p. 57 amused me especially. But "collaboration with the powerful" is not always the cleverest way. In 1933 it was certainly better to be "enslaved to a rock."

After a long period of indisposition, an abscess in one of my lungs was verified by means of bronchoscopy, and it became necessary to operate without delay. This was done in Chicago by a master in lung surgery, Dr. [William E.] Adams, and succeeded perfectly. Now, of course, I am subject to all sorts of precautions and limitations, but at the same time I am not really unhappy that my constitution has had to undergo this testing. For it has passed *cum laude*. The doctors say that a man of thirty could not have come through the affair with more composure. Well, of course, if one were a squealing child, one couldn't have achieved what is after all there and will not be blown away so easily.

Yours,
Thomas Mann

1. I can no longer recall what newspaper clippings these were.

2. *Prometheus: Das griechische Mythologem von der menschlichen Existenz,* Albae Vigiliae, N.S. IV (Zurich, 1946); new ed. in *Rowohlts Deutscher Enzyklopädie,* 95 (Hamburg, 1959) (*Prometheus: Archetypal Image of Human Existence,* trans. R. Manheim, Bollingen Series, LXV:1 [New York, 1963]).

Mann to Kerényi

Dear Professor,

The new gift has been received with gratitude and deep respect.[1] Much underlining! I was particularly glad about the Callimachus paean and the Chrysaean symbolism of arrow-snake-shot-bite.[2] Certain things I make my own immediately, or rather they are recognized and appropriated for the task at hand.

Warmest greetings! All my letters now are this short.

Yours,

Thomas Mann

1. "Apollon-Epiphanien," an offprint from the *Eranos-Jahrbuch*, 13 (1945), 11–48; reprinted in *Niobe*. See Mann to Kerényi, February 7, 1949, note 1.

[2.] Cf. *Doctor Faustus* (New York, 1948), p. 393 (*GW*, VI, 521 f.).

Kerényi to Mann

Tegna, August 1, 1946

Dear, honored Sir,

I was deeply touched that in spite of the serious disruption your illness caused, not only for you personally but also for your work, you have responded now with a second note to the material I sent you, even to the less important "Apollon-Epiphanien." I have also suffered in this period from something almost as grievous as an illness, which occasioned a fairly long interruption of any real work. It was, as I now realize, an unavoidable humanist's ailment, the ailing existence born of isolation; its cause lies in the fact that one had adopted the standpoint of the persecuted and oppressed, but not because one had the misfortune to belong to them—no, I did not have that misfortune—but simply on the grounds of humanity. Whenever "fortune" and "misfortune" are reversed in the course of world history, the humanist invariably remains alone: those who were formerly in misfortune may move from deliverance to power, but the humanist will have nothing to do with "power." Nor would he be condemned to impotence. He wants to work effectively, but it is just this possibility that the powerful of the time will hardly grant him without requiring a *sacrificium intellectus*. He is then forced into isolation, and they attempt (not this or that party but all parties, not only the Communists or the capitalists, but *all* who are in possession of power), as if in fun and without malice—to starve him to death.

This is the situation that leads one to doubt the possibility of a "humanism for its own sake," of service to mankind and to the cause of humanity without allegiance to any seat of power, be it party or mighty state, and makes one almost acknowledge that, on the basis of history, there exists only a court humanism—as in the fortunate position of Goethe in Weimar, to cite a great and thus also a pure instance, a lofty, isolated phenomenon. You know his attitude on letter writing: "When I see that people write to me only for their own sake, that their aim involves their own personality, then I have nothing to do with it," etc.[1] This impresses one all the more today when so many letters await an answer at the cost of creative work. Undoubtedly, the instrument of the spirit may not be troubled and diverted with *quisquiliae* [trivialities]. And yet I cannot help but regret what proved to be for German culture, for all mankind, a fateful characteristic of withdrawal in

Goethe, an absence of humanistic participation. Goethe's lack of feeling for a *res publica doctorum virorum* [commonwealth of learned men], whereby he might have extended the republic of the humanists into an undertaking shared by the poets as well, appears to me today as the tragic supplement to the devouring isolation of other great Germans: notably, the cases of Hölderlin and of Nietzsche. An archipelagic harmony of island voices—what a humanistic concert might this have produced; instead, what came was, at best, only a late, not undistinguished poetic as well as humanistic sectarianism!

And this leads me to speak of a book (I have now overcome my "ailment," not without resignation but, as it seems, in accord with my destiny, and what still remains on the level of "practical" difficulties need not be discussed here)—a book that pleased me immensely because it correctly brought together the essential elements of post-Goethian German humanism (I dislike to put "humanisms" into numerical order): H. A. Maier's *Stefan George und Thomas Mann* [Zurich, 1946]. The afterword, admittedly, betrays a certain intimidation. [. . .] But the author's daring, though it seems subsequently to have awed him a bit, does break up the outmoded compartments of orthodox literary theoreticians and, in place of their embittered but on the whole quite "trivial" stylistic criticism, makes the "individual," the person, once more the criterion of literary scholarship. Furthermore, I am grateful to him for a quotation from your volume of essays in English, *Order of the Day* [1942], about which I had not known at all. The passage shows to what an extent what I wrote in the letter on humanism[2] at the end of *Die Geburt der Helena* (". . . he will possess a fearless knowledge of the dark, demonic, radically natural side of man along with a sense of piety, etc. . . .") grew out of the same fundamental conviction to which you yourself came. I consider this one of the most moving confirmations of our mutual contact. Now, following this line of thought—namely, instead of the bankruptcy of a "Goethe posture" in the name of humanism, the necessity for a reciprocal connection between a purely poetic position and a serious, secular-religious humanistic attitude—I come (finally) to a passage in your last long letter [February 12, 1946], one which I only yesterday transmitted to a German poet who was active in the Dutch underground movement. He recalled something you had said (in Noordwijk, in 1939) about an esoteric period that would come only after the war. But didn't you write in that letter that "only if humanism moves toward the religious . . . can it acquire the binding force necessary to bring together the dispersed human race around a new source of authority"? In view of a book like H. A. Maier's and the activities of a [Wolfgang] Cordan in the Netherlands, one is tempted to ask how "such an ideal gathering based on a sense of community and of piety," of which you also speak in that letter, could become a reality. Not for the sake of some "esoteric teaching," but rather, oriented in self-evident, clear terms toward the idea of "man." As a preliminary I thought of a kind of humanistic "colloquium on religion" to be organized next year in Switzerland or Holland . . .

But here I am forced to return to the beginning of this letter and raise the other, much more urgent and general question (not a personal one at all in this context): Is a solidarity among the humanists themselves possible, those humanists who take upon themselves a solidarity with the persecuted and then —aside from the solidarity of the persecuted themselves—stand alone; or are the humanists themselves reduced to nothing but —urbanity? Did you not write somewhere that Goethe combined the demonic with the urbane? Thus what would be missing in him would be precisely what connects and commits, the dimension of the humane and of sympathy? Can this be the reason why no humanism could derive from him? These are questions with which I am deeply occupied and which I convey to you "between ourselves." For, in spite of the experiences that lie behind me, I still envisage the ideal of a solidarity among poets and humanists—a kind of "catholicism," but without pope or dogma. A new spiritual forum needs to be created, beyond the province of the academies (I have just learned today that I have been elected to the Hungarian one) or of the press, whose power to annoy is incalculable (I enclose a sample)[3]—an academy that Goethe perhaps might have founded *after all* if *Weimar* had not existed. And *Weimar no longer exists.*

With warm greetings,

Yours,
K. K.

[1.] Kanzler von Müller, *Unterhaltungen mit Goethe,* ed. Ernst Grumach (Weimar, 1956), entry of April 24, 1830. (Professor Bernhard Blume kindly provided the source of this quotation.)

2. "Grundbegriffe und Zukunftsmöglichkeiten des Humanismus" (*HSF,* pp. 368–382). See Mann to Kerényi, February 12, 1946, note 1.

3. A clipping from a Swiss newspaper that contained an inconsiderate reference to Thomas Mann's *Betrachtungen eines Unpolitischen* (see Introduction, note 17) and a copy of the letter that I sent to one of the editors.

Mann to Kerényi

Pacif. Palisades, Calif.
September 15, 1946

Dear Professor Kerényi,

I was very pleased to read your letter of August 1 and am most grateful for your loyal efforts to shield me against certain trivial acts of meanness, which it would perhaps be better to let pass with nothing but a friendly smile toward the perpetrators. The fact that I acknowledged certain Romantic-Protestant-nationalist attitudes thirty years ago and stood for a "spiritual" Germania against the Expressionist pacifism and activism of the time[1] seems never to lose its fascination for certain scribblers; they are repeatedly given to bringing the matter up again, and I might even view this compulsion regarding my moral biography in a flattering light. Now certainly it goes a little too far to draw parallels between my position of 1914–1918 and ——'s odious pro-Nazi pronouncements of 1933, and then to find excuses for both one and the other. Really, this pleases me not at all. It was possible in the last war, by virtue of one's basically German education, as a disciple of Goethe and Nietzsche, to view the other side's Jacobite-puritanical rhetoric with a certain irony. But *not* to recognize immediately such infernal garbage as German National Socialism for what it was, but rather to speak of it at the start in quite different, most distressing terms, was, I think—less excusable, though I find it decidedly tiresome to keep bringing this up against that great scholar.[2]

I wish I could enter more fully into the rich store of ideas in your letter. I must admit that I have always viewed that saying of Goethe's about correspondence which you cite with a sense of cheerful sympathy and approbation. Most letters that lay claim to our eyes and thoughts remind me in the end of that scene the Munich comedian [Karl] Valentin used to play: he enters as the joiner Bramstätter and says: "Good day, your honor! I have come with regard to, about—*me*." All have "aims involving their own personality," and to find a letter writer whose aim is solely to give pleasure, a selfless individual who does not simply exploit and strain one—this takes time. I do not wish to justify Goethe's reserve. I understand it all too well and have much of it myself. But I know that Goethe, like all our great ones, like Luther, Bismarck, and Nietzsche, was a stupendous ornament for Germania but at the same time, as a formative force, a dire fatality. I sought in *The Beloved Returns* to convey a sense of this in all its "apprehensive" comicality.

What I said regarding the necessity for a humanism experienced in the religious sense and of a *gathering* based thereon came from the heart. The nations should be summoned together to withstand what a blind, raging impulse of mankind is about to commit. Who would have thought that after this war, which all decent men considered a struggle for humanity and human freedom, all the forces of political inanity and depravity would combine to celebrate such orgies! I shall never leave any doubt as to where I stand, but I am not made for congresses and discussions, and it seems to me that the academy of your dreams will be possible only within a World Government,[3] which will itself remain a dream for a long time yet—although it is being dreamed in very precise fashion and prepared for eventual realization in the greatest detail by a group of well-intentioned men here in this country. This is happening in Chicago, of all places.

I have, of course, received Dr. Maier's book to read—and have confined myself to perusing certain parts. My feeling about such exertions is, "Why not? Let them do as they please." I too find that some of his remarks reveal a humorous anxiety. Good heavens! If my mother had brought me into the world to be a pathos monger and unbending prophet—I would have cut as fine a figure, I suppose, as [Stefan] George.[4]

Yours sincerely,
Thomas Mann

[1.] In *Betrachtungen eines Unpolitischen*.

[2.] Probably C. G. Jung. See Manfred Dierks's dissertation "Studien zu Mythos und Psychologie bei Thomas Mann," p. 285; and cf. Mann to Anna Jacobson, February 22, 1945, in Thomas Mann, *Briefe, 1937–1947*, ed. Erika Mann (Frankfort on the Main, 1963), p. 413.

[3.] In English in the German edition.

[4.] See Kerényi to Mann, August 13, 1934, note 5.

Kerényi to Mann

Tegna, November 27, 1946

Dear, honored Sir,

When I received your letter of mid-September I was rereading *The Beloved Returns,* which accompanied my rereading of Goethe's conversations, and thus the letter signified no "outside interference" in my train of thoughts but an extension of them toward the possibilities which are very close to realization for you. The academy of my dreams! You properly called it this. I could also call it the "academy of dreamers," those dreamers who dream the eternal dreams of mankind and anticipate the dreams of other men . . . I never had "congresses" in mind (I have just returned from one, an international congress of "philosophers" held in Rome, which granted me not a single new idea, but something else: the opportunity to see this most beloved of cities once again) or discussions. I thought of real meetings and confrontations, of attentive, hearkening association during the day and the still continuation of thoughts, of dreams during the night, about what the philosopher had heard from the poet, the poet from the philosopher, and the philologian from them both. It was something eminently Pythagorean that I had in mind, something akin to the cloister—not precisely in the sense of *The Glass Bead Game* (yet how significant it is that this noble and disciplined dreamer has anticipated just *this* dream of ours!), but rather something less "in the head," though for heaven's sake not "*gemütlich,*" something born of a dedication to the spirit, the spirit that inspires in diverse ways but is always fructuous and generative . . .

[148]

This dream is perhaps a primal European, certainly also a primal Asiatic, one. If indeed that "World Government" which, you say, is being dreamed in very precise fashion in America, should ever assure us of the kind of freedom you discussed (also in a precise fashion) in your PEN Club speech (in Stockholm, I think),[1] why should not such "un-American" dreams as the one I have indicated also be realized? One hears many complaints in Europe today about a world-wide "Americanization," but I think there is something to be said for the American who, when he saw the ruins of Rome, asked, "Why haven't they ever rebuilt all this?" (an anecdote current in Italy these days). What excuses him is a characteristic which, incidentally, is also typical of the English, namely, his freedom from envy. At least they will not disturb our dreams because of envy. At this stage it is certainly not easy to find a form for this "academy of the catacombs"—I think often about this matter and that is perhaps its most proper "form" at the moment: that a few individuals still think about it.

I can write you something very hopeful about another idea on which I meditated in a very compressed and pressed letter to you [December 19, 1945]: about a theory of the divine as a theory of man, about a "Greek mythology for grown-ups" for which all my works up to now would serve as preparation (also the preparatory dreams). The opportunity for this comes from America in the ideal form of a fellowship from the Bollingen Foundation (41 Washington Square South, New York 12). I have given you the address because the administration of the foundation itself indicated in a most friendly and confidential manner that one of the conditions for obtaining the fellowship would be a few lines from individuals —and your name came up—who know my writings and view them favorably. The point, of course, would be to indicate that something may be expected of me in consequence of this fellowship: some work—in fact, precisely this mythological one

—which could then appear in the Bollingen Series. The series already includes H. Zimmer's *Myths and Symbols in Indian Art and Civilization* [New York, 1946] and similar titles of a psychological-mythological orientation, among which a book of mine would represent no alien element. May I request some such words from you, to be addressed to the administration of the Bollingen Foundation? I dare ask this because such a grant would not represent any interference with my destiny, though it would affect it decisively, but something that had come about organically, a "dispensation" in the full sense of the word.

My devoted greetings.

Yours,
Karl Kerényi

[1.] "Das Problem der Freiheit," delivered in Stockholm, September, 1939 (*GW*, XI, 952–972).

Mann to Kerényi

Pacif. Palisades, Calif.
January 1, 1947

Dear Professor Kerényi,

The year has come to a close, but alas without my having thanked you for your friendly letter. But I do not want the first day of the new one to pass without doing so, even if it has to be in such a scanty fashion, with a little note [*Blättgen*], as W. Goethe used to spell it in his youth.[1] In my old age I shall have to make do with such little notes, at least for the time being, since I am putting all my energy into the completion of this monstrous novel that has already occupied me for two and a half years and should reach its final stage this month—the most personal, the most daring in more than one sense, and for me the most exciting of my books [*Doctor Faustus*]. But now, never again a novel! For the rest of my life only short things that can be managed within a foreseeable period. *Buddenbrooks, The Magic Mountain,* the Joseph stories with the interpolated Goethian play of the gods [*The Beloved Returns*], and now this—quite enough high structures for one lifetime and surprisingly many for mine. I have had patience—which Schopenhauer called the true form of heroism. The noble man! He felt that his one-and-all, what he faithfully held fast to, was already heroic. Most enchanting, but from there it all went up to Nietzsche into icy regions—and then frightfully fast and deep down . . .

I am just imagining and composing the work with which my musician will take leave of his spiritual existence: the symphonic cantata "The Lamentation of Dr. Faustus" (following the *Volksbuch*),[2] a most expressive work since it is a lament, for this certainly constitutes the origin of all expression and every expressive act is essentially a lament. As soon as music, at the start of its modern history, had emancipated itself into expressivity it became *lamento* and *Lasciatemi morire.*[3]

Now, "lament" strikes a very contemporary note, don't you think? Things look very bleak. The news reaching me from Germany, particularly, is so hopeless. Of course, at heart I believe that, all in all, mankind has been pushed *ahead* a good bit, in spite of all signs to the contrary. And it is, after all, a tough beast. Even the A-bomb does not make me seriously concerned about it. Hasn't it demonstrated its toughness in each of us? Is it a singular frivolity or a blissful sense of confidence that allows us still to create *works?* For whom? For what future? And yet a work, though it be one of despair, must in its essence always be grounded in optimism, in a faith in life—and it is a strange thing about despair: it already carries in itself the transcendence to hope.

And with this paradox about the *work,* I have naturally come to *your* work, the "theory of the divine as a theory of man" [November 27, 1946]. It must and will be written, and I consider it a great joy to be able to do something to help bring this about. I am just in the process of drafting the letter about the fellowship. It will be much better to send it directly to the foundation rather than all the way to Europe first.

My little note has after all become two. I shall add only my warmest wishes for the New Year.

Yours,
Thomas Mann

[1.] For *Blättchen,* the diminutive of *Blatt.*

[2.] The *Faust Book,* printed in Frankfort on the Main in 1587, the source for all subsequent treatments of the Faust theme.

[3.] "Let me die," the title of an aria (also a madrigal) by Claudio Monteverdi (1567–1643). It attained enormous popularity in the seventeenth century and became a model for musical forms of lament in the period. This passage is almost identical to one in *Doctor Faustus,* pp. 485 f. (*GW,* VI, 643 f.).

Kerényi to Mann

Tegna, March 4, 1947
Lauro e Fontana

Dear, honored Sir,

Here it is already March—though not yet spring, as in other years—and I can only now send thanks for the stimulating New Year's letter and also for that other letter about which I heard soon thereafter! How often was that New Year's letter on the chimney piece read over again, and each time it conveyed something of the excitement of which it speaks. What excitement may we not expect from the work itself (which I trust has been brought to completion in the meantime) if the "author's account" alone can arouse one so!

You know my weakness for stimuli of this sort. It was almost exactly a year ago that I communicated to you the joy that came to me from the belief—or the illusion—that the publication of our correspondence had contributed something to the maintenance of this humanistic heritage, to the very possibility of intellectual excitement. To those who then conveyed to me their sense of excitement I could now add others. But since everything is so hopeless, as you write, in the German, and *not only in the German,* areas of Europe, what is required is an exceptionally intense stimulus of this sort: a convulsion. And *this* is what I expect of Adrian Leverkühn. Perhaps it is naïveté, but it is nonetheless the same belief in the life of mankind that the author had when he created the work.

And your "Nietzsche," so long awaited, which I understand we may soon *hear* directly from you! Can one seriously hope for this? Has my small Plato reached you—and found a reception—by now?[1]

I close with greetings and deepest gratitude.

Yours,

Karl Kerényi

P.S. I have an uncertain feeling that a letter of mine of a year ago[2] has never reached you, so I enclose a copy—for the sake of historical completeness, although the alternatives mentioned therein are still not resolved . . . My daughters have already been here and have returned to their positions in Hungary.

[1.] See Kerényi to Mann, June 4, 1947, note 5.
[2.] February 26, 1946; included above.

Mann to Kerényi

1550 San Remo Drive
Pacific Palisades, California
April 10, 1947

Dear Professor Kerényi,

"Some things are lost in the night," we read in that magnificent poem of Eichendorff, which Schumann set just as magnificently; its conclusion is the moralistic warning, "Take care! Stay awake and alert!"—which simply asks too much and is not meant seriously at all.[1]

I only wanted to say: I have your letter of March 4, but you did well to include a copy of the one of February 26, [1946], with its gratifying remarks about the correspondence, since it was altogether *new* to me, and, to my distress, I know nothing of a Plato either. It is primarily printed matter, heaven knows why, that gets lost so easily these days. We anticipate sailing on May 9 on the "Queen Elizabeth" to England and then expect to be in Zurich soon after the 20th. The Nietzsche lecture —well, yes, I am bringing it along.[2] In writing it out I touched, fleetingly, on half of what needs to be touched on—and wrote twice as much as I shall be able to deliver. What remains will thus be a little *thin*. Furthermore, it was primarily conceived for an American public, so contains too much information for you seasoned Europeans. All this to bring down your expectations a few notches.

The Bollingen Foundation has sent me a most friendly, in principle hopeful, acknowledgment of my recommendation. Auf Wiedersehen!

Yours,
Thomas Mann

[1.] The poem is Josef von Eichendorff's "Zwielicht," which concludes: "Manches bleibt in Nacht verloren— / Hüte dich, bleib' wach und munter!" (*Werke*, ed. R. Dietze [1891], I, 14). Mann cites the same poem in "Das Lieblingsgedicht" (*GW*, X, 922), a brief essay responding to the query, What is your favorite poem? The last line of the poem is used as a motif in *Doctor Faustus;* see pp. 77 and 499 (*GW*, VI, 106, 662).

[2.] See Kerényi to Mann, June 4, 1947, note 2.

Kerényi to Mann

Tegna, near Locarno, May 28, 1947

Dear, most honored Sir!

Mr. Basler[1] writes that you have at last arrived in Zurich. Let me send my most cordial greetings! Your last letter, with the news of your trip to Europe, awaited me here as I returned from Italy—I hope that by tomorrow I may already be able to express in person my joy at your arrival. My usual "tour of duty"—in the service of the gods of my destiny—takes me to Zurich on Thursday and to Basel on Friday. I return to Zurich on Saturday morning, but will be occupied by some tiresome official matters until noon. Thus I shall come to your hotel on Thursday—when, I believe, you will receive this letter—between 4:00 and 5:00 to inquire when I may see you.

The following week should follow the same rhythm for me: in Tessin Sunday through Wednesday, when we celebrate my Lucia's seventh birthday (she was born in the seventh year of the correspondence), and Thursday–Saturday in northern Switzerland.

Once more, greetings and welcome.

Yours,
K. K.

[1.] Unidentified.

Kerényi to Mann

Tegna, June 4, 1947

Dear, honored Sir,

Let me send you my congratulations on this June 6 and also
this document I mentioned during our recent meeting, the first
review of our correspondence to appear in Germany, presumably in the Berlin periodical *Athena*,[1] hitherto unknown to me.
I received it indirectly and without details. It is in a certain
sense a belated tribute to your 70th birthday. The current one,
the 72d, seems part of a veritable festive cycle. It began for me
with our reunion and reached its climax yesterday with your
lecture.

I heard the Nietzsche lecture[2] on the radio from beginning
to end and want to say, briefly and to the point, what impressed me particularly in it. First of all, of course—this is
connected with the remark I made in our conversation regarding that passage of your *Leiden an Deutschland* which raised
an issue of the greatest contemporary significance[3]—your allusion in the introduction to the "new humanism"; and then the
fact that you immediately provided an exemplary demonstra-
tion of it: I mean that first part of your talk, which seemed to
me, at least in terms of its intent and precision, a kind of
"medical procedure" that isolated and circumscribed the ailment by surgical means.

And the consequence (as well as the condition) of that
opening was the quality of humanity, indeed of piety, that
showed itself in the fairness with which you set forth the issue.
This quality undoubtedly derives from a deep, an almost famil-
ial association with that fateful child of the great bourgeois
century, and it sustained you where the medical impulse alone,

even in its fullest development as in Freud, would have fallen short. You were thus able to lay bare the "crudest" and the most dangerous of all misapprehensions with a precision and clarity that could not be bettered, unless perhaps by adding this remark: if Nietzsche had been understood from the "aesthetic" and not the "ethical" side, if he had not been interpreted in a puritanical, Reformation sense as a "moral reformer," then he certainly would not have caused any damage. Nietzsche reached by way of the Reformation—this is what brought about, not the most noble but the most atrocious acts of world history . . .

Please forgive these comments, which I allow myself partly because toward the end of your talk the same idea of a nonpuritanical, un-Protestant humanism came to me, an idea that I had expressed in my letter in *Centaur*,[4] which I trust you received yesterday together with the Plato.[5] There I put the question as follows: "What has become of those religious energies of the Middle Ages which were subsequently made to serve a Protestanism opposed to the imaginative and formative faculties?" Today I would perhaps put it this way: "Where may these energies be directed, and in what forms, after having served the ruling powers, the forces of evil in Germany and elsewhere?" To "man" is your answer, and mine, in the form of a "new humanism." But I would close now with a formula, a definition from that speaker whose spirit you exemplified yesterday, the spirit of the *"old humanism,"* the Ciceronian: "Vir *bonus,* dicendi peritus."[6]

With warm greetings,

Yours,
Karl Kerényi

[1.] By Günter Blöcker, *Athena,* 1947, pp. 29–33.
[2.] "Nietzsche's Philosophie im Lichte unserer Erfahrung" (*GW,* IX, 675–712).

[3.] Excerpts from a journal for the years 1933 and 1934, published privately in Los Angeles in 1946 (*GW*, XII, 684–766).

4. Wolfgang Cordan's periodical in Amsterdam. The letter was in *Centaur*, 2 (1946), 158 ff.; reprinted in *Deutsche Beiträge*, 4 (1949), 119 ff.; and as "Lob des Konkreten" in *Apollon* (*HSF*, pp. 383–388).

5. *Über Liebe und Unsterblichkeit: Die Sokratischen Gespräche Gastmahl, Phaidros, Phaidon,* with an introduction by Karl Kerényi (Zurich, 1946).

[6.] "A good man, skilled in speaking" (Quintilian 12.1.1). The sense is that unless a man possesses moral integrity he cannot pretend to the skills of a speaker.

Kerényi to Mann

Tegna, June 13, 1947

Dear, honored Sir,

I can imagine how overwhelmed you are with mail these days when many of the Swiss are just rediscovering you; indeed, many of the younger generation who may still have been inclined a short time ago to share some of the resentment against the "deserter of his homeland" are making a veritable "discovery." And yet—in fact, precisely because I assume that the response your voice has long since called forth in other countries has finally made itself felt in Switzerland too—I cannot withhold expressing my great pleasure in reading about your address to the students in an article of the *Neue Zürcher Zeitung* entitled "I Turn to the Youth," and I must add my regrets that I was not present.[1] I knew nothing of the event and devoted that day to a meadow high in the Alps and to two little-known authors: Florus, to whom the "Pervigilium Veneris" is probably correctly ascribed, and Aristippus, in whom the concept of *humanitas* (*anthropismós* in Greek) occurs for the first time.

Certainly, such an "idyllic" element, the preservation of this possibility of human existence, *also* belongs to the humanist creed; its realization may be called the joint achievement of Nietzsche *and* Walter Pater (the fusion of the two raises aestheticism to a piety free of arrogance). Yet it will clearly not suffice for that "new humanism" which you stressed more than ever before. And I am very glad that in your talk you put the chief emphasis on "intricacy," "the nobility of the human spirit"—and of course its freedom!—the *"mysterium* man," and the new humanism as a "humanism of knowledge" (if the newspaper account I read is correct). (Let me add that I am particularly touched by this correspondence: the book on Socrates that I am planning is intended as nothing else than an exemplification of the sentence on which I have so long meditated: "We are mysteries.") [. . .] But I wonder whether the young people [. . .] understood that the inexhaustible object of a "humanism of knowledge" is precisely the *"mysterium* man," and [. . .] that it requires the most intensive investigation? How much I would like to see your text—and be witness to its success! Is there a copy I might read?

Tomorrow we go to Montagnola, then Sunday through Wednesday I shall be in Tegna again, and Thursday I begin the usual trip through Zurich to Basel. We shall be staying in the vicinity of Zurich with friends from the 21st until about the end of the month (in Herrliberg, with Dr. Hans Bänzinger).

With warm greetings,

Yours,
K. K.

[1.] "Ansprache an die Züricher Studentenschaft" ("Address to the Students of Zurich") was given June 10, 1947 (*GW,* X, 367–371).

Mann to Kerényi

Baur au Lac
Zurich, June 15, 1947

Dear Dr. Kerényi,

A thousand thanks for your letter. I can hardly respond to it, as I am exhausted from celebrations, activities, all sorts of agitation. There were two lectures in Bern with much to-do. I found the city delightful once more. Yesterday we went to the *Götterdämmerung*—a strange experience. A mad German conductor [. . .] presided over the downfall, and very impressively. Tomorrow we are obliged to go to Basel and then, as I said, a few weeks in Flims, Graubünden, where I shall have more work than rest. There is still a visit to Holland before we return "home" at the end of August. In the meantime, if at all possible, there may come a visit to Tessin, to Montagnola— perhaps an occasion to see you once more. Otherwise, next year. I take my leave, then, for a short time or longer, and please keep me informed of your activities!

Yours,
Thomas Mann

Mann to Kerényi

Grand Hotel Surselva
Flims-Waldhaus, June 26, 1947

Dear Professor,

Thank you for the impressive package![1] Though I am swamped with proofs, I immediately read your letter in *Cen-*

taur and find that you have very successfully taken a stand against "nominalism" or a fetishism of the name, in defense of a new or renewed humanism. My God, it is simply *sympathy* that must be the basis of everything, so that it may become not a sermon but life. The obnoxious neighbor—yes, certainly. But I always have to think of Goethe, who knew men and yet could say that what released him from melancholy was always the sight of a human face. Your Plato piece is a possession that promises very much indeed.

After long months of agitation we are so happy to be here in the midst of the peaceful woods, but an endless task, left far behind me, must be worked at once more, and to rush through the whole novel in this fashion, red pencil in hand, affects me deeply. Meanwhile the dear Germans buzz and sting unceasingly all about me; it became so nasty at one point that I was forced to send a letter to the American *Neue Zeitung* in Munich.[2] They are all half-crazy there, which is understandable.

All the best to you and to your work!

Yours,

Thomas Mann

1. See Kerényi to Mann, June 4, 1947, notes 4 and 5.

[2.] Published July 7, 1947 (*GW,* XI, 793–795). Mann responded to a charge that in 1933, after his departure from Germany, he had sought permission from the Nazi regime to return. The charge was wholly false, as could subsequently be proved. See Hans Bürgin and Hans-Otto Mayer, *Thomas Mann: Eine Chronik seines Lebens* (Frankfort on the Main, 1965), pp. 210 f.

Mann to Kerényi

Dear Professor,

How grateful I am for your profoundly learned paean to Mother Nature, or Dame Physis,[1] though I have little affection at the moment for her frightful cynicism, in which I agree to a great extent with Blake, who thought, "Whoever believes in nature cannot believe in God, for nature is of the devil."[2] Very true! There is a filthy swindle in it all. And that monstrosity of the cosmic All measured in billions of light-years, to which one can as readily say "Let it be!" as "Hosanna!" arouses not the slightest sense of awe in me. My reaction, like Goncharov's to the rising ocean, is "What a nuisance!"[3] Of course, *physis* is the prerequisite of the spirit; beauty comes from it too, and since one is engaged in creating, one should not be against the "creations." In any case, your study is as stimulating as any you have written, and those early, struggling speculations of mankind about becoming and being, as well as the outbursts into poetic, hymnic song when the speculations can go no further, have something very moving in them.

It appears, unfortunately, that I shall not see you again during this European stay. The visit to Tessin was originally planned in connection with one to Stresa, by way of Mondadoris, from which we have just returned. But the Hesses were not and are not in Montagnola. We met them in Lucerne while they were on their way to Wengen (it was a most pleasant, friendly day), and now we shall fly on the 10th directly to Holland, where I have lectures again, and then on the 29th we shall make our way home from there. I am altogether too exhausted for Tessin (partly on account of the heat)' *and* too busy: I must still write a preface for a new collection of prints of Masereel,[4] whose visit gave me great pleasure just recently.

So it must be farewell for the time being. If the world still holds on to the kind of peace it now "enjoys" I shall come again next year.

With all best wishes,

Yours,
Thomas Mann

1. "Die Göttin Natur," offprint from the *Eranos-Jahrbuch,* 14 (1946), 39–86; reprinted in *Niobe* (see Mann to Kerényi, February 7, 1949, note 1). *Physis* is the Greek concept of nature. On Mann's view of Mother Nature see Introduction, p. 23 and note 32.

[2.] The source in Blake could not be located.

[3.] In "Voyage with *Don Quixote,*" Mann recounts this incident: "Ivan Goncharov was once on the high seas during a violent storm. The captain had him fetched from his cabin to behold it: Goncharov was a writer, he said, the storm was magnificent, he ought not to miss it. The author of *Oblomov* came on deck, looked about him, and said: 'Yes, it's a nuisance, isn't it?' And went below again" (*Essays of Three Decades,* p. 430; *GW,* X, 428).

[4.] *Jeunesse* (Zurich, 1948), a volume of woodcuts by Frans Masereel. Mann's preface is in *GW,* X, 783–789.

Kerényi to Mann

Tegna, August 5, 1947

Dear, honored Sir,

Since there was no opportunity this time for a second meeting—I had been prepared for that by word from Hesse that you were to meet him in Lucerne—let me at least pass on this personal news which reached me in official form today and for which I am deeply grateful to you and other friends who have done so much to further my labors: the Bollingen Fellowship has been awarded me for two years. [. . .]

I have heard that *Doctor Faustus* will already appear in the fall. Is this true? I am very impatient. And "Nietzsche"? And the address to the Zurich students? Forgive me! People ask me; they are eager to know—including

Yours,
K. K.

Kerényi to Mann

Asklepios[1]

November 7, 1947, Lauro e Fontana, Tegna (On leaving for a visit to Budapest, where my address will be c/o K. Lukács, Budafoki-ut 55, until December 15, 1947.)

Yours,
K. K.

[1.] The same illustration is in Kerényi's *Asklepios: Archetypal Image of the Physician's Existence,* p. 99, with the following caption: "Asklepios on a winged snake as a sun god flaring up out of darkness. Medal of Alexander Severus (A.D. 222–35), from Nikaia, Asia Minor." See Introduction, note 28, above.

Mann to Kerényi

1550 San Remo Drive
Pacific Palisades, California
November 26, 1947

Dear Dr. Kerényi,

My thanks for the page with the lovely symbol! And my best wishes for your homeward trip! Is this to be a serious effort to resume old ties, so that I may look to Budapest as the site of our next meeting?

I am doing nothing but listening for echoes of *Doctor Faustus,* which is just putting some pens in action in Switzerland. I still cannot get over the fact that this book, which is essentially a secret work, should now really be a public matter for European readers. In fact, something of the excitement which, in spite of and along with its tediousness, is after all the essence of the book vibrates in the reviews. You will not recognize in it the mythological colleague of the Joseph stories. However, if I ponder it well—perhaps you will.

Best wishes and greetings!

Yours,
Thomas Mann

Mann to Kerényi

1550 San Remo Drive
Pacific Palisades, California
July 17, 1948

Dear Dr. Kerényi,

Welcome back to Tessin and warm thanks for the generous form of your greetings to your ever appreciative reader! If you call me "master," I may well call you teacher and supporter, for every one of your works that I have yet seen has proved to be not only instructive and stimulating but also, as you know, useful in some way for my own dreams and constructs. I am convinced that this will also be the case with "Urmensch und Mysterium,"[1] a piece that seems to be related to a sphere of interests familiar to me from your earlier work. There have been times when, on receiving something new, I said to myself, "This is probably of no special concern to me," and even put off reading it. And then when I began to read, it turned out to concern me after all; I paid attention, began to underline, and quietly the productive machine began its work.

After such a long pause in our exchange there is more to report and say than can fill a letter. I regret that as a result of your absence you missed the appearance of my *Doctor Faustus* in Switzerland and the deep impression the book has produced there. I have never heard any work of mine spoken of with such keen accents. This applies to Germany too and even to this country, where the translation has still to appear. I have, since completing this synthesis and recapitulation of my small world, done some other things and broached new paths. But

[166]

whatever I accomplish henceforth can only be an epilogue and pastime.

With warmest greetings,

Yours,
Thomas Mann

1. An offprint from the *Eranos-Jahrbuch*, 15 (1947), 41–74; reprinted in *Niobe*. See Mann to Kerényi, February 7, 1949, note 1.

Kerényi to Mann

Tegna, September 11, 1948

Dear, honored Sir,

You are very right, I regret to say, about the long pause in our exchange, an unusually long one in these so-called days of peace. And you have guessed the chief reason—my travels: first to Hungary during November of the past year, where a letter of yours did reach me; then more than once to Rome, where I received the letter in which you welcome me back to Tessin (and our family, is in fact, still encamped in the same valley); finally, immediately after my last return from the south, a flight to Amsterdam, where the International Congress of Philosophy would have opened with my lecture "Menschen in griechischer Anschauung"[1] if, thanks to the reluctance of French authorities to grant me a transit visa, I had not arrived too late. I was no less delighted, though, with the intention of the organizers of the congress, which became clear to me when I arrived, and my return to that unchanged city of the canals moved me almost as much as did—two years ago during the previous congress—my return to Rome, which has since given so much to my intellectual life. Thus gradually I become less ashamed to call myself, now and then (though, of course, never "professionally"), a "philosopher."

Nevertheless, I did not miss the appearance of *Doctor Faustus* in Switzerland. In fact, it was I who first brought the news to Hungary. When, in the course of a radio interview in Budapest, I was asked whether I was still in contact with you and when I had last seen you, I replied, not by speaking of personal matters, but of *Doctor Faustus*. [. . .] The winged serpent as a symbol of the divine healer Asklepios that I sent by air to you was meant as a sign of the fact that I—read. Read and read, and I shall continue to read without entertaining the hope that I shall ever get to the bottom of all that is concealed, in fun or seriousness, in this—how would you have me put it in good old German? *"Öffentlich Geheimbuch"*[2] [open secret book]—in these secret yet open *confessiones*. What moved me most deeply—so much so that I have not fully recovered from that emotion to the present day—I could not, of course, reveal in that interview. And I do not know whether I can reveal it even to you. Sometime, perhaps, in a conversation or in an extended secret-public study. Let me only say for the moment what I do *not* believe: that what you will still write will "only be an epilogue and pastime." I *still* expect something significant from the author of *Doctor Faustus*.

With warmest greetings,

Yours,
K. K.

1. Reprinted in *Niobe*. See Mann to Kerényi, February 7, 1949, note 1.

[2.] An allusion to "öffentlich Geheimnis" (open secret), a phrase frequently used by Goethe, e.g., in the poem "Epirrhema," *Werke* (Hamburg, 1956), I, 358.

Mann to Kerényi

1550 San Remo Drive
Pacific Palisades, California
September 12, 1948

Dear Dr. Kerényi,

For a long time I had no copies of my Faustus novel, and
meanwhile there was your trip to Hungary. Thus there never
seemed to be an opportunity to send you the book, though I
have all this time been conscious of the fact that you, who so
often treated me to the fruits of your intellectual labors, should
actually have been among the first to receive one. Now that
the printer has provided me with a few copies, I can finally
send one to you, and it is only to inform you of this that I
write these lines.

The *Joseph* lies far behind, and the paths each of us follows
are no longer as close as in the period of its conception. But
what I once wrote you [February 16, 1939] concerning the
novel about Goethe [*The Beloved Returns*]—might it also be
mythology?—this applies finally also to this novel of pain, even
though it lacks the mythical gaiety that suffused the "humoristic song to mankind." But then a book of the *end*—and *Doctor
Faustus* is that—how could it be gay! I can only hope that his
terrors are still lighted by a glimmer of art and thus *after all*
of gaiety.

I hope you find yourself in the best of health and produc-
tively engaged.

Yours sincerely,
Thomas Mann

Kerényi to Mann

Lauro e Fontana, Tegna
November 2, 1948

Dear, honored Sir,

Our letters went off almost on the same day; yours reached me in Rome, and when I returned here a few days ago, I found *Doctor Faustus* waiting for me at the post office, just as I had imagined it. For me this is both moving and comforting. To have trust in the life of the spirit is to have trust in the realization of what is beyond our calculation and control, and a realization of this sort constitutes continuing evidence of those most delicate threads which tie men to one another and to the sources of creativity.

This trust, so richly repaid through the arrival of the *Faustus,* makes me hope that you will not have misunderstood my letter. It is really not easy to develop what I intimated there. And since the present letter is to be only a first expression of gratitude, I still do not know how to begin with the essential issue. Let me say first of all that, since the conclusion of the Joseph novels, our paths have diverged only at *one* level, and that not the deepest. In fact, your way in that respect had been a separate one from the start, while at the deepest level we were both concerned with the same aspect of humanity, namely, what I have called in mythology, the lupine-Apollonian. The mythologist, however, was and is, alas, a sufferer from migraines, with ample and quite conscious experience of illness, an observer from both his own standpoint and that of others of the phenomenon and its variants—not excluding Hesse's *Steppenwolf*—at the level of both cultural history and personal biography, whether his own or that of individuals

[170]

close to him. I have looked at the matter in association with important physicians and psychologists with whom I am friendly, notably with Dr. Szondi, and we have explored the problem of illness as a spur to intellectual activity at a deeper level than merely the bacteriological.

Let me state this directly too: the example of so many truly great figures at the end of the last century who were subject to syphilis—you will undoubtedly know of the tragic case of Ady through the Hatvanys[1]—involves a factor that complicates any clear evaluation; it represents only the historically conditioned *fin-de-siècle* costume of an eternal human tragedy whose clear outlines, painful yet instructive, are thereby more obscured than not. Since your novel is also a social document, you could not avoid precisely this kind of costume. But you can imagine how directly—both in human and intellectual terms—your statement of the problem affected me. How childish I find the enthusiasm of some professors of aesthetics or literary history who have finally discovered the great artist that lies in Thomas Mann now that he has advanced beyond what only yesterday was called "art" into a nameless spiritual sphere in which—to cite only one of the many new judgments—poetry and music no longer meet through rhythm and melody but by virtue of some "insight into . . ."! As confirmation of our continuing, unconscious companionship along the same path, let me find for you the issue of the Swiss *Musikzeitung* (September 1946, I think) in which I illustrate the problem of breakthrough or outbreak as a mode of healing, with reference to Bartok's *Cantata Profana*.[2] Thus I have not been unprepared for a more profound understanding of poor Adrian Leverkühn, and I shall convey to you as much as I can of my thoughts on the subject.

Let me now only send you warmest greetings and thanks.

Yours,
K. K.

[171]

[1.] Endre Ady (1877–1919) was a major Hungarian poet who had contracted syphilis and made it one of the themes of his work. Lajos Hatvany (1880–1961), a Hungarian writer and liberal political figure, had been a friend and supporter of Ady and was an acquaintance of Mann.

[2.] See Mann to Kerényi, December 30, 1948, note 2.

Mann to Kerényi

December 30, 1948[1]

Dear Professor,

Please accept this brief note of thanks for your most recent, excellent packet; I read it through with the greatest interest. I could not help but admire your versatility as I read the essay about the *Cantata Profana,* for me the most interesting piece —not that I intend anything against wolf and goat![2] Warmest good wishes for the New Year.

T. M.

1. This letter is written on the verso of a photograph of Mann in the garden of his house in Pacific Palisades, California.

2. "Über Béla Bartoks Cantata profana," *Schweizerische Musikzeitung,* 86 (1946), 325–328. "Wolf und Ziege am Lupercalienfest" first appeared in *Mélanges de philologie, de littérature et d'histoire anciennes offerts à J. Marouzeau* (Paris, 1948), and then in *Niobe.* See Mann to Kerényi, February 7, 1949, note 1.

Mann to Kerényi

1550 San Remo Drive
Pacific Palisades, California
February 7, 1949

Dear Professor Kerényi,

Wonderful things of yours have come my way again: the

rich Niobe book,[1] in which I rediscovered with pleasure some familiar pieces, and then from Ciba in Basel the glorious volume about the divine physician,[2] among whose lovely illustrations (an incorrect subordinate construction)[3] I was especially delighted to meet again Telesphoros, the little hooded figure. Very new for me was the at least partially Roman conception of Apollo as Apollo Medicus.[4] Of course, the associations of the far-shooter with illness *and* its cure are perfectly evident. Remarkable too the changing views of the outer features of Asklepios—from a Zeus type to a Hermes type. Is the youthful form the archaic one?

I am very happy to see that your status both as scholar and author is in the ascendant and that you are able to establish a secure position in Europe.

I proceed in the old manner, moving ahead slowly with one project or another. At the end of April, after a long quiescent period, we fly off once again. The obligatory Goethe lecture takes me first to the Middle West and the East, then to England, Sweden, and finally, at the beginning of June, I trust, to Switzerland. Hopefully, you will not be out of the country just then!

Yours,
Thomas Mann

1. *Niobe: Neue Studien über antike Religion und Humanität* (Zurich, 1949).
2. *Der göttliche Arzt.*
3. Thomas Mann's comment is between the lines.
4. Apollo the physician.

Kerényi to Mann

Tegna, June 16, 1949

Dear, most honored Sir,

I am extremely grateful to Dr. Leisinger[1] for having made

[173]

possible our meeting in Küsnacht the day before yesterday by means of his automobile. I met this charming couple only recently during a trip in Italy. It was amidst an eminently classical landscape—not too far from "your" Palestrina—that I learned that they were zealous admirers and even acquaintances of yours, and furthermore, readers of our correspondence.[2] Since then they have attended the lectures I gave in Zurich, not only at the C. G. Jung Institute, but also for a small private group. They informed me that you were giving a lecture on the very evening I was. I finished early, but even so we arrived at the Sonne only at ten—I for my part more a passive than an active participant on this surprising occasion, somewhat bewildered by the recollections of the visit I paid you in Künacht in that oppressive year 1937.

In addition to the reunion itself—and a reunion precisely in Küsnacht—something else turned out most happily that evening. Who knows better than you how important it is that the recounting of the purest intellectual experiences, those that are free of any outside influences, must come about in a propitious manner! I have for a long time held back revealing to you such an experience regarding *Doctor Faustus*. Now I can say quite simply: why? There evolved in my mind a thesis about the work that seemed too esoteric even to me, the thesis of a historian of religion and psychology who ventured all too boldly into the field of literary criticism, though of course he was one who had always eagerly explored religious issues, even in their most secularized forms. The thesis derives from what one may call, in the most general terms, the fundamentally somber and earnest tone of the novel, a quality which, in my view, marks it as a Christian work of extraordinary significance, transcending any denominational bounds. It seemed necessary to me to establish such a view quite thoroughly before expressing it to the author, much less to a larger public. Thus I awaited an occasion to speak to you, while confining

[174]

my public statements to *the* field in which I felt more competent.

The first thing, then, that I learned in Küsnacht was that you are undertaking—if I may put it in a somewhat dry, diagnostic fashion—a *manifestly* Christian theme, the story of a sinner, penitent, and pope [*The Holy Sinner,* 1951]. How your treatment will be judged from a denominational viewpoint need not concern us here. But I found confirmation of my thesis in this flowering of a seed that could already be found thematically and organically in *Doctor Faustus,* and also in the fact that your first reaction was far from negative. Of course, I shrank at first from your suggestion that I deal with the work from my standpoint. The task you set me seemed too weighty and responsible. Now, as I peruse the notes that I made in reading the novel, I no longer find it so impossible to attempt an assessment from the perspective that I have in mind. This would also involve the role of migraines—apparently *only* a medical consideration, but one that is of general significance in view of the many great migraine sufferers in our cultural history.

And now that a dialogue about *Faustus* has begun between us, it would be well-nigh irresponsible of me if I did not put this question to you: Whence comes your knowledge, not only *concerning* migraines, but *of* migraines, of that atmosphere and those secret relationships among migraine sufferers that I could not help noting and confirming? And now yet another, quite practical question: Where can one find an eminent publication, not merely literary or scholarly, that could serve as a worthy medium for the kind of free and serious humanistic considerations that I have in mind? For the *Neue Schweizer Rundschau,* I have already agreed to do a review of the new edition of the *Mutterrecht.*[3] The German periodicals are still too regional, and the French and English as well are *nearly* regional . . . I am not quite sure that it will be possible to get the answers to these questions from you personally in the

[175]

coming weeks: after the Tuesday lectures I go to Biel and Bern. The following week begins with Basel, and after Zurich, though not immediately, comes Trogen (an interpretation of the Aegean festival scene for the Goethe celebration). A message to Tegna will always reach me.

June 18, 1949

In rereading the above I feel great regret that I failed to write you from this perspective much sooner, notwithstanding the fact that what you might more normally have expected from the "mythologist" was an assessment of the melancholy warmth and gaiety that are concentrated in the figure of the humanist. And I appreciated all this fully, though silently— this warmth and this gaiety mingled as they are with the *tristitia humanistarum* [melancholy of the humanists] (a concept that I should have coined long ago). And with what foolishness you have had to put up in the meantime! I mean principally the reproaches of the composer who has perhaps forfeited the right to be named in a serious exchange between us.[4] That something like this could even come up publicly! Naturally, since it is a public that remains as good as unaffected—not to mention *influenced!*—by any endeavor to achieve a true science of man and humanity.

On the other hand, we can probably thank this barbarous state of affairs, it seems to me, for your small novel about the origins of *Doctor Faustus,*[5] something of no small significance in the contemporary scene; so far I have only seen the first installment, but even that is delightful to read! The whole will be of the greatest relevance for me. Let me add this as my excuse: I was waiting for, as you must know, *the* sequel to *Doctor Faustus*—whatever the "delivered one" might be called and whatever historical form his "deliverance" might take. This inner sense of waiting and expectation was resolved in

the fortunate encounter of the Küsnacht evening, and that
sense of good fortune still remains with me.
My grateful and cordial greetings.

Yours,
K. K.

[1.] Unidentified.

[2.] Mann spent the summer in the town of Palestrina in 1897, when
he began work on *Buddenbrooks*. He situated a major episode of *Doctor Faustus* there: Adrian Leverkühn's interview with the devil (chapters xxiv–xxv). See Kerényi's essay "Thomas Mann und der Teufel in
Palestrina," *Die Neue Rundschau*, 73 (1962), 328–346; reprinted in
Tessiner Schreibtisch (Stuttgart, 1963).

[3.] Johann Jakob Bachofen, *Das Mutterrecht* (1861), ed. Karl
Meuli (Basel, 1948).

[4.] Arnold Schönberg, in a letter to the *Saturday Review of Literature*, 32 (January 1, 1949), had protested against Mann's delineation of
the twelve-tone technique of composition in *Doctor Faustus*. Schönberg
feared that posterity would tend to associate the method with Adrian
Leverkühn, the hero of the novel, or with Mann rather than with
Schönberg himself, its originator. Responding in the same issue of the
magazine, Mann rejected the charge. But to satisfy Schönberg he subsequently added a brief note at the end of the novel formally giving
Schönberg credit for the twelve-tone system. Mann's letter is in *GW*,
XI, 683–685.

5. *Die Entstehung des Doktor Faustus* (Amsterdam, 1949) (*The
Story of a Novel: The Genesis of Doctor Faustus* [New York, 1961]).

Mann to Kerényi

Zurich, Baur au Lac
June 20, 1949

Dear Professor Kerényi,

Many thanks for your letter, which supplements and reinforces our recent exchange in such a happy manner. It was delightful that you managed the meeting—and in just that place —with the assistance of Dr. Leisinger, whom you are not alone in liking and cherishing. I admire your decisiveness and adaptability, in which I am all too wanting. You did not miss much in that fragmentary lecture I gave. All the more important to me was our brief talk, which was nonetheless full of substance regarding both your affairs—your situation in the world and in Hungary—and my own. Your remarks about the religious, Christian character of *Faustus* struck me and gave me a sense of satisfaction that comes with the truth. It certainly *is* true and almost self-evident; how, after all, could such a radical book not somehow reach into a religious sphere? Nonetheless, it has been called "godless." That shows the intelligence of people whose profession is to write about "belles-lettres." Thus my exclamation *"You* should write about that!"—which was intended, not as a bare solicitation, but as a contingent wish and thus not altogether seriously. But naturally this theoretical wish takes on substance as soon as you, quite independently, indicate the serious possibility of its realization. If you have the time, the desire, the impulse, if you consider it *not* as a dilettantish, unscholarly departure but view the book as somehow within your sphere, then nothing would be more interesting to me than a statement by you on the subject—to me personally, first of all, but to many others too, I believe, even if they do not see their own experience in that of the reviewer.

The question of publication is of course of secondary importance, but that does not prevent it from being difficult enough. Something about the book has appeared almost everywhere. I still do not see any solution but realize quite well that you would need a specific prospect. The matter must be considered. The French edition will appear only next spring. I wonder whether one should anticipate it. The Italian is just about to appear—so perhaps a periodical there? But it seems to me that the article, if you write it, must certainly also appear in German. Let time bring counsel; the two really do seem to go together.

Yours sincerely,
Thomas Mann

The American-sponsored *Monat* in Berlin might be a good idea.

Kerényi to Mann

Biel-St. Peterinsel
June 23, 1949

Dear, most honored Sir,

Your kind letter has not yet reached me. My wife told me of it yesterday on the telephone, and thereupon I tried to call you—in vain, for you were in conference and I had to proceed immediately. And since, unfortunately, I will no longer find you in Zurich next week, let me only say, as a matter of principle, that I am not against any German public—in other words, that I am *open* for Germany. And, wishing you well on your journey, I'd like to tell you what occurs to me in this island atmosphere. Two years ago, in the course of his postwar journey, Martin Buber suddenly asked me, quite unexpectedly, at the small station in Tegna, "Would you accept a professorship in Germany?" I was unprepared for this and asked him in turn, "Would *you* accept one?" To which he responded, "How old are you?" "Fifty." "If I were fifty, I would still risk that adventure." He then returned to *his* homeland, to Jerusalem, and held out through the most difficult period of the new state. But what he said about Germany was undoubtedly patriotic, though not only for Germany but for Europe, neither optimistic nor pessimistic but humane and realistic—an attitude

[179]

which, if Buber holds it, I can certainly see as a possibility for myself.

I wish you a good journey and look forward eagerly to seeing you again.

Always yours,
Karl Kerényi

Kerényi to Mann

Pontebrolla, near Tegna
December 25, 1949

Dear, most honored Sir,

I cannot let the year end without sending greetings to you. They come again from a different house, though one that is not very far from the earlier "tent," which I can see from here. But it is precisely the instability in the external sphere that allows one to experience all the more intensely the recurrences in the internal one and in the intangible relations about us. I sit here today reading a book that captivates me almost in the same way *The Magic Mountain* once did, one that seems to radiate in my direction from the same pole as that other—I mean Viktor Mann's book.[1] How *abundant* is the source of your life if absolute strangers can draw sustenance from it, as from a fountain of youth, *a whole life long!* Has *your* new book appeared yet? And, in the midst of my Greek, mythological labors (I am at work on my "mythology for adults"[2] for an Anglo-American publisher), I draw courage and strength from another polar opposite—Buber's unique "chronicle," *Gog and Magog* [Heidelberg, 1949]. Thus my greetings for the New Year in both the old and the *new* spirit.

Yours,
K. K.

[1.] *Wir waren fünf.* See Introduction, note 32.

2. I undertook the projected "theory of the divine as a theory of man" by proceeding in two directions: first, a faithful recounting of the Greek material ("for grownups," as I put it in my letter of November 27, 1946) in the books *Mythologie der Griechen* and *Heroen der Griechen* (see Introduction, notes 10 and 12); second, monographs such as *Hermes, Prometheus, Asklepios,* etc.

Mann to Kerényi

1550 San Remo Drive
Pacific Palisades, California
January 4, 1950

Dear Herr Professor,

My warm thanks for your New Year's message—for one of "my" years; *Buddenbrooks* appeared in 1900, *The Magic Mountain* in 1925, and shortly I shall be 75. I may speak in this fashion since you are occupied just now with "our" myth, the faithful book of my deceased brother. In Germany its effect has been nothing less than conciliatory. "Yes, when one reads that and sees things from the human side, one finds that the Manns are actually charming people." It is most amusing.

I wonder whether we shall meet this year. Albin Michel[1] is most insistent that I come to Paris in the spring for the appearance of the French version of *Doctor Faustus.* In that case we would of course again spend a number of weeks in Switzerland. But I am *at least* as sick of allowing myself to be toasted as to be abused and think sometimes that I shall stay nicely at home in 1950.

I am occupied just at the moment with your "Urmensch und Mysterium," one of the most remarkable things you have written. It concerns me in connection with my Gregorius, especially his nourishment on the cliff. Hartmann von Aue[2] describes this in a manner that is *just barely* reminiscent of the Epicurean hypothesis regarding *uteri*[3] of the earth and the sustaining milk they at first provided for man. With the aid of your citations about the "sluices" I intend to develop this more accurately and more fantastically than does Hartmann—who would undoubtedly open his eyes in amazement if he read my rendering of the story.

All the best for your well-being and the success of your project!

Yours,
Thomas Mann

[1.] Mann's French publisher.

[2.] Hartmann von Aue (c. 1165–c. 1215), medieval German poet whose short epic *Gregorius* was a primary source for Mann's *The Holy Sinner.*

[3.] Wombs. In the essay "Urmensch und Mysterium" (in *Niobe,* p. 56), Kerényi quotes at length from Lucretius' *De rerum natura,* Book V. The German translation that Kerényi uses renders *uteri* in line 808 of Lucretius as *Schläuche,* the word Mann uses in the relevant passage of *Der Erwählte* (*GW,* VII, 192). The English version, *The Holy Sinner,* trans. H. T. Lowe-Porter (New York, 1960), p. 247, has "sluices."

Mann to Kerényi

Dolder Grand Hotel
Zurich, July 5, 1950

Dear Professor Kerényi,

"Zeus und Hera" is again most interesting.[1] I had never realized in my innocence that they were brother and sister, though this sort of union is perfectly familiar to me from Egyptian sources. It has probably always been connected with a claim to the most exclusive nobility, in which "equality of birth" ceases right after the sibling stage. In my rendering of the Gregorius tale [*The Holy Sinner*], in which, incidentally, the themes are indicated only lightly, I unconsciously endowed my delicate little sibling pair with the conviction that, because of their refinement, only they stood on a level of equality with each other.

Very convincing too the idea of "ambivalence" of judgment as both superhuman and strictly forbidden. Altogether, the essay testifies to astonishing learning. The combination of sensitivity and erudition is always extremely fascinating.

My wife is recuperating very well from her operation, though she is still at the Hirslanden Clinic. We shall be able to bring her up to Sils Maria in about a week.

I have been worried, confused, and nervous for some time but am now beginning to work again.

Yours sincerely,
Thomas Mann

1. "Zeus und Hera," *Saeculum,* 1 (1950), 228–257.

Mann to Kerényi

March 9, 1951[1]

Behind this latticed window I am again reading much Kerényi, happy in the knowledge that the labyrinth does have an exit[2] and living gladly with the exalted, somewhat dissolute family.[3]

In May, I trust, we shall again be in Switzerland—perhaps even for a longer time.

Before that you will be receiving the story of the good sinner Gregorius.

Warm greetings!

Thomas Mann

1. This letter is on the verso of a photograph of Mann's house in California.

2. An acknowledgment of the second edition of *Labyrinth-Studien.* See Kerényi to Mann, November 15, 1940, note 3.

3. "Die olympische Götterfamilie" ("The Family of Olympic Gods"), *Paideuma,* 4 (1950), 127 ff.

Kerényi to Mann

Ponte Brolla, May 28, 1951

It is the expectation, dear, honored sir, the expectation of your arrival and that of *The Holy Sinner,* that has delayed until now my thanks for your kind card with the, as it now seems, already "used up" house in California. (How many such latticed husks of our existence must be lived through, used up in an age like ours that puts Heraclitus to shame!) But *your* (in Latin, your genius' [guardian spirit's]) day approaches once more with a firm and festive step, and so may these lines celebrate the god and the man of that day, *ubi ibi*[1] —expectantly, for (to cite an oracle that came to me once from an old Chinese wisdom book) "You may move the city, but not the well!"

With my wife,

Ever yours,
K. K.

1. "Wheresoever."

Kerényi to Mann

Most honored Sir,

The experience of *The Holy Sinner* was again something incredible—indeed, the most incredible that has ever been granted me by an author. For it is certainly incredible that an author should grant one in later years the same sensation of novelty, of intellectual daring, and of artistic triumph as he has twice already in a lifetime, first in youth and then in the critical years of maturity. Did Goethe with the *Wahlverwandtschaften* [1809] perhaps have a comparable effect on certain readers, probably only few, who had once been overcome by *Werther* [1774]? The similarity is suggested also by the audacity of the two works, though I think that with the *Wahlverwandtschaften* Goethe surpassed everything conceivable in his day more through an audacity of content than of language, while here content and language, both daring in the extreme, are intermingled as certainly never before in German literature, not to mention the literature of *our time*.

My own experience I can only convey by means of another superbly described literary (though surely, not *only* literary) experience—and could I, an "alien" too, offer anything better? I mean the famous scene in the Bibliothèque Nationale: "I am seated and read a poet. There are many people in the hall, but one does not feel them. They are in their books. Sometimes they move within the pages like men who are asleep and turn over between two dreams. Oh, how good it is to be among reading men. Why are they not always thus? You can go over to one of them and touch him lightly; he feels nothing. And if you jostle a neighbor slightly while getting up and ask his pardon, he nods toward the side where he hears your voice, his face turns toward you and does not see you, and his hair is like the hair of one asleep. What a comfort that is. And I am seated and in possession of a poet. What a destiny. There are now perhaps three-hundred people in the hall, reading; but it is impossible that each one possesses a poet. (God knows what they possess.) Three-hundred poets do not exist. But look now, what a destiny: I, perhaps the most impoverished of these readers, an alien—I am in possession of a poet. . . ."[1]

While reading *The Holy Sinner* I felt continually *this* intensity of awareness: *"I am in possession of a novelist,* an epic fabulist, perhaps the very *last,* certainly the only one still remaining, and it is already enough, more than enough, to experience this unhoped for, this unforeseeable good fortune and contentment. . . ."

I could observe the same contentment in the facial expressions of others who read the book—my wife, for one—and in the statements of friends. But I am proud also *to possess this awareness* ("What a destiny"), thanks to the preparation of a life devoted *only* to the highest and deepest calling of the mind, and the certainty that I have here again encountered what is at once most primordial and most advanced, recognized and admired it in the full exercise of my knowledge and critical powers, but also with an admiration that is content to be wholly in harmony with its object.

All this would lead me to many particulars if I did not feel the need to send these lines off immediately, though I do so somewhat at random since I do not know where you are staying. But perhaps you are in the very countryside in which I now find myself, though I am soon off to Austria for a short time.

Always yours,
Karl Kerényi

[1.] Rainer Maria Rilke, *Die Aufzeichnungen des Malte Laurids Brigge,* Insel Edition (Leipzig, 1920), Part I, p. 52.

Mann to Kerényi

Dear Professor Kerényi,

A word of greeting from this beautiful, comically overrun spot and a thousand thanks for your letter of the 10th. I am very, very glad that you like *The Holy Sinner*. On September 7 we return to Zurich (Waldhaus Dolder) for a number of weeks. Sometime, somewhere I hope still to see you.

Yours,
Thomas Mann

1. A postcard from Bad Gastein, Austria.

Mann to Kerényi

Zurich, Waldhaus Dolder
September 23, 1951[1]

Dear Professor Kerényi,

Many thanks! Am reading the *Mythologie* like a boy. It is a good idea to send both editions to California.[2] We fly already on the 29th. I shall certainly write some heartening words to Thames and Hudson about *The Gods of the Greeks*.

All the best to you both.

Yours,
Thomas Mann

1. A postcard.
2. *Die Mythologie der Griechen* (Zurich, 1951) and the same work

in English translation, *The Gods of the Greeks*. The publishers Thames and Hudson received a kind letter from Thomas Mann recommending the work to the English reading public; his recommendation to the German public appeared in *Weltwoche,* December 14, 1951 (*GW,* X, 929 ff.).

Kerényi to Mann

Pontebrolla, Tessin
February 19, 1952

Most honored Sir,

I should not be at all surprised if my *Mythologie* and all the fuss and bother it involved, including your own exertions on more than one occasion, were now quite blotted from your mind, leaving only a sense of my ungratefulness in writing to you so tardily. What has happened is that I have meanwhile also undergone surgery and can consider myself enriched by this experience on the operating table—especially since it occurred without a general anaesthetic and I could observe in the face of a lovely woman the fascination of an incision, an intervention into living tissue. In fact, this just concluded (as I hope) adventure constituted only the last stage of an odyssey that took me to Scandinavia and Finland, from there to Rome and Assisi (to an Apollonian discovery),[1] and then back again to Germany—in spite of the readings and lectures (or perhaps just on account of them), a period of extreme passivity from which I am only now beginning to rouse myself for expressions of a more personal nature.

The copy of your testimonial to the English reading public arrived here between the northern and the Italian trips. What made me so happy was not new to me—I knew it already from that card you sent from Zurich about your first reaction to the *Mythologie*—but it confirmed the fulfillment of a great, life-long ambition: to repay *some* of my joy, though with what immense assistance (the assistance of the Hellenes!), to the author to whom I have been indebted for the purest enjoyment ever since my youth—the kind of enjoyment a boy gets from a storyteller, a mentor; and at the same time to lead the primordial impulse of narration back to the point where it is no less at home than in its most ancient sources! This is perhaps a man's greatest joy: to be able to repay felicity with felicity, no less in spiritual and intellectual terms—far from it —than in bodily. Yes, it is precisely this: to be able to offer at least a trace of gratitude in that highest sphere where man partakes of divine gifts. For this I am, of course, once more *indebted*, indebted to the Greeks, as you said in the *Weltwoche*, in that second testimonial that caught me completely by surprise; it reached me in Rome through the agency of kind Dutch friends, who were much more overjoyed about this than anyone, even the best of friends, could possibly have been in Switzerland.

But the success then came precisely in Switzerland, a success beyond all expectation, irrepressible; the book dealers "would never have believed it"—with a Greek mythology!!—and now they are already asking for the *Heroes of the Greeks,* which must naturally follow once I have completed the "Mysteries of the Greeks."[2] The effect in England was almost the very opposite of what I had expected. Robert Graves,[3] whom I had hoped to repay, not for anything very great but for his amusing work with its touch of unconscious genius, came forth, as if in the grips of jealousy, with a truly hysterical outburst against the book. Old John Cowper Powys, that Celtic magician about whom we exchanged views many years ago, confesses in a letter to the publisher, "I have not read a book for years which I've found more exciting or more provocative or fuller of suggestions, in my most favourite of all studies" (thus I did repay *him*). And a professional colleague who recently

[189]

published *The Greeks and Their Gods* [London, 1950], W. K. C. Guthrie, "Reader in Classics in the University of Cambridge," praises the book in all sincerity—this I had not really expected—with expressions like "I had no idea that Greek mythology," "a new and startling impression," "some salutary shocks." Finally he quotes the passage from "Freud and the Future" about the pleasure in mythology that comes in late years[4] and supports it with words of *the old Aristotle,* which I give in his translation: "The more I am alone and thrown back on myself, the more I become attached to myth."[5]

A happier conjunction between a sage of antiquity and one to whom one can write and express one's gratitude can hardly be imagined! Let me thus close my account and letter of thanks, but not without adding the wish, no new wish certainly, that the sage I mean may soon and permanently be settled close by. It is possible that my wife—whose warmest greetings I transmit to you—may be able to write you something specific on this matter. For now only the *ricordi* [souvenirs] (snapshots by the Italian waiter!) from Lugano!

Yours sincerely,
Karl Kerényi

1. Published in *Symbolae Osloenses,* 29 (1952), 110–113; in *Unwillkürliche Kunstreisen,* pp. 12 ff. (*ASM,* pp. 68 ff.). See Kerényi to Mann, October 13, 1954, note 2.

2. The order was reversed, the *Heroes* (1958; English, 1959) coming before *Die Mysterien von Eleusis* (Zurich, 1962).

[3.] Graves (b. 1895), English poet, novelist, and writer on mythological subjects. Kerényi's reference may be to *I, Claudius* (1934) or to *The White Goddess* (1948).

[4.] See *Essays of Three Decades,* p. 422 (*GW,* IX, 493).

[5.] In the German edition the quotations from Powys and Guthrie are in English.

Mann to Kerényi

1550 San Remo Drive
Pacific Palisades, California
March 20, 1952

Dear Dr. Kerényi,

Now it is *my* turn to thank you—for your kind letter of thanks. There was nothing to thank me for! The little testimonials, both the English and the German, were set down easily and with pleasure. They are really of no great significance, their principal aim being to make the public eager. In reading your work I could never help but think of the old book of mythological tales that had already served for my mother's schooling and for which my taste as a boy was unquenchable.[1] It had a Pallas Athena on the cover and, with its accounts of the deeds of Hercules and the battles of Zeus, took the place for me of all stories of Indians. The "diamond-honed sickle" that Zeus drew against Typhon impressed me particularly. "This forced the brute to yield!" It is now 67 years since I read and reread that sentence, and I think that I shall still recall it in the hour of my death.

"Let us look kindly on the hospitable one who shields the stranger from insult." The hospitable one—no one in the third class at school knew who that was—except me! Thanks to that reading experience of my childhood not one of the creatures, noble or horrific, in your book was unknown to me, at least by name, not even such as found no place in the "Classical Walpurgis Night"; and as I read about Tethys,* I recalled that after *The Holy Sinner* a German teacher had written me that *what I must now do is complete Goethe's "Achilleis" in the form of a prose novel.*[2] Do you find that such a silly idea? I, not at all. But of course there remain the Krull memoirs that I have set my heart on bringing to completion; and yet, in spite of the comical nature of the subject matter, they have a tendency to degenerate into a "Faustian" strain. I must consider myself happy if I can still drain *that* sea. One cannot, after all, do everything. But I would not lack ideas even if I reached 120. It is too bad for them, for the Achilles or the Erasmus novel, for example. For who else is capable of it?

What! You were operated on? Why? What for? But never mind! You have long since gotten over it, embarked on distant journeys, announced exciting new plans. With respect to the assessments of *The Gods of the Greeks,* you may rest assured that Powys is more significant than Graves.

I wanted to tell you: I am preparing a German edition of my essays: *Altes und Neues: Kleine Prosa aus fünf Jahrzehnten* ["The Old and the New: Shorter Prose from Five Decades"].[3] For in fact the material extends over a period from 1906 to 1952 and includes all kinds of things from the volumes of essays, now unavailable, in the first complete edition of my works, also pieces from the time of the struggle against Hitler —and the most recent things. There will be a section of letters in which I would also like to include my letters to you from the years 1934 to '41, since they would enhance the autobiographical character of the whole. I trust you have nothing against that? [. . .]

The kind *camerière* [waiter] had already also sent me the *ricordi.* May the occasion be repeated soon! We still have no idea when we can get away from here.

Yours sincerely,
Thomas Mann

* But I confuse this with *Thetis,* the Nereïd! (T. M.).

[1.] The book is Friedrich Nösselt, *Lehrbuch der griechischen und römischen Mythologie* (Leipzig, numerous editions from 1844 on). See Dierks, *Studien,* p. 237. Mann mentions the book in similar terms in a brief autobiographical essay, "Kinderspiele," first published in 1904 and again in 1922 (*GW,* XI, 329; bibliographical note, p. 1151).

[2.] Goethe, in 1799, wrote only one canto of the projected epic poem. He later thought of turning it into a novel but never took it up again.

[3.] Frankfort on the Main, 1953.

Kerényi to Mann

Ponte Brolla, April 17, 1952

Dear, most honored Sir,

I hope my wife's letter will have served to excuse the lateness of my own. I am thankful and proud to know that the most valuable letters of our published correspondence will now also appear in a volume of yours. I have also informed Dr. Brody in Lugano, the publisher of *Romandichtung und Mythologie,* of the matter, and naturally he immediately gave his approval. [. . .]

And what a full letter I have to thank you for! (My own was rather confused and the operation mentioned therein [. . .] of no importance; but who knows? Who is familiar with the positive and the negative possibilities of his own nature?) The "degeneration" [*"Ausarten"*] (isn't the root *ars, artis?*)[1] of Krull in a "Faustian" manner, the possibilities of an Achilles, of an Erasmus epic! Yes, who else would be capable of it? For my part, of course, the Achilles novel would be the more exciting and stimulating . . . The fact that Thomas Mann as a boy was so greatly affected by a book of mythology certainly holds a deeper meaning (which only I, perhaps, have sensed thus far)! It could, after all, have been something else—but the potential resonance, the fundamental orientation of sensibility, was already there precisely *for that*. What a tremendous "homecoming" that would be—an Achilles epic! And assuredly an authentic one. He who has not experienced an enthusiasm in which laughter and tears are mixed has never been allowed to perceive the Achilles of the *Iliad!* But I can well imagine that he would reveal himself to you, his way prepared by Tonio Kröger[2] and the young Joseph!

I too can speak of a sort of homecoming; you can well imagine what, since you know of my voyage to Greece. I found that I again enjoyed the cooking, redolent of mutton fat; the spicy, bitter retsina wine; the language with its native peculiarities, which I thought I had forgotten long ago but which came back to me—enjoyed it all so much, in fact, that I was able to realize how much at home I had come to feel 20 to 22 years ago in that country which knows how to compensate the hardships of life with such gifts, as for example—and to whom could I better transmit the latest literary, and at the same time mythological, news from Greece than to you, all the more since it deals with Archilochus?[3] It involves an inscription—discovered by the Greek archaeologist J. M. Kondoleon, who is about to publish it—carved on the poet's tomb, which was erected, by consent of the Delphic oracle, inside the temenos of Apollo and the Muses on Paros. The tale goes—quite in the spirit of my own *Mythologie,* which is most gratifying[4]—that once, as a boy, Archilochus was sent by his parents to take a cow to the market in town. On the way he met a group of maidens (probably nine), who teased the youth and suddenly disappeared—with the cow. They left in its stead a lyre lying on the road. Could we wish for anything more Hermetic?

Yours sincerely,

K. K.

1. "Art." The etymology is of course not meant seriously.

[2.] The hero of Mann's story *Tonio Kröger* (1903).

[3.] Greek iambic and elegiac poet of the seventh century B. C.

4. My study of this, "Die Dichterweihe auf Paros," may be found in *Griechische Miniaturen* (Zurich, 1957), pp. 87–94 (*ASM,* pp. 250–255).

Mann to Kerényi

Zurich, September 22, 1952[1]

Dear Professor Kerényi,

What pleasure I had with your sublime causerie "Der erste Mensch," ["The First Man"][2] so intense and serious at the start and so comical in its conclusion! A lovely, delightful piece!

I had occasion to talk to your kind wife recently after a lecture. She had no difficulty, either, in detecting all kinds of mythical matter in my jesting.

I must put together a small talk about [Gerhart] Hauptmann, for Frankfort, for the ninetieth anniversary of his birth. I'd rather do something else but am, as it were, *obligated*.

Yours sincerely,
Thomas Mann

1. This letter is on the verso of a photograph of Mann in the midst of his family at the breakfast table.
2. In *Der Psychologe*, 4 (1952), 242 ff.; and in the little book *Umgang mit Göttlichem* (Göttingen, 1955).

Mann to Kerényi

Erlenbach-Zurich
February 7, 1953

Dear Professor Kerényi,

I have really been terribly remiss toward you. A number of books have arrived—two in any case—from the publisher and from you, and I have hardly been able to look into them or to thank you—which is only partly owing to mislaying your address in Tessin, but chiefly because I have been tired, troubled, and depressed for some time already. After the trip to Germany and Austria, where I contracted a serious case of bronchitis, there was the move from the hotel to this house and the arrival of our things from California, which are not easy to accommodate in our much smaller quarters here—the installation of my library, especially, caused absurd difficulties. All these problems, many still unresolved, have been most distressing. Further aggravating my nervousness are the many letters I owe and a diminished energy for work, which has resulted in my not being able to finish a story that had been going quite well up to a point, though it is now stuck. In short, things go badly.

Going out at night is not good for me, all the more since getting the car down in the heavy snow here is something of an adventure. Nonetheless, I have agreed to attend a premiere at the Schauspielhaus (Shaw's *Pygmalion*). This is on the 12th—and two nights in a row are too much for me. Thus I shall not be able to hear your lecture,[1] but I console myself with the thought that I have less need of it than the students you will be addressing. They will have much that is new to experience, but I am spoiled and jaded by my involvement with your writings.

Consideration is what I require now. Basically, the cause of it all is that the readjustment to central Europe after twelve years in California has been more difficult for my system than I had expected. Add to that the world situation and the odious side of man's nature that it brings to the surface. I am often sick of it, though healthy enough to make any death wish comical. Also a dilemma!

Auf Wiedersehen until a favorable hour.

Yours,
Thomas Mann

[196]

1. The lecture was "Titanismus und Humanismus in der griechi-schen Mythologie," sponsored by student associations of both universities and by the C. G. Jung Institute in Zurich.

Kerényi to Mann

Ponte Brolla, February 17, 1953

Dear, most honored Sir,

You put me to shame—and not for the first time. For there is no doubt that of us two you are the better correspondent, thanks to the superb discipline of your work habits, whereby a Goethian tradition is maintained with Olympian composure high above the distracted heads of poor stragglers like myself. How inconsiderate I have been toward you; alas, how incon-siderate I have been forced to be! Only my wife was able to attend your reading from *Krull* last September, and it was something like a punishment to get her detailed account of it and of her conversation with you! I was punished still more in not being able to hear *Der Künstler und die Gesellschaft* ["The Artist and Society"],[1] which also came at a time when I felt that I had to make full use of my stay at home. Thus I was forced to swallow all the sand through which the dutiful news-paper reports filtered the water from the purest of springs. Well, at least the faint strain of the longed-for voice gives all the more joy to the yearning reader . . .

Thus your voice has reached me in recent days only by means of dear and not so dear intermediaries, unless, that is, I consider a great and unexpected experience a form of "hear-ing," for I *hear* you (ever since Budapest, at the Belvárosi Szinház, where I saw and heard you for the first time) when-ever I read you. I refer to a renewed encounter with *The Magic Mountain* on a lovely October day, in a period of recollection and recovery that has been in progress ever since my trip to Greece in the spring. It was then that I began the "inventory" of my most treasured inner possessions, which I perhaps opened to public view too soon and which will not let me rest.

This renewed encounter, which really took place immediately after my return to Greece, must be credited to the book guild, which made the book accessible again, and in such a welcome manner, including even an "introduction to *The Magic Mountain*" by the author himself ("welcome" is no empty word, coming from an exile who has been forced to reassemble his library!)—thus endowing the book with a new and valuable bonus even for me.[2] In this period of retrospection (the first ten years of our stay in Switzerland are just coming to a close), I can assent with all my heart to your idea that it is necessary to be reminded of oneself! During these days too the publishers sent me the last copy of the *Griechisch-orientalische Romanliteratur*—another renewed encounter—which reminds me that I must soon return to questions about the novel (and then also to *Doctor Faustus,* for which I have not yet summoned up courage, but also to *The Transposed Heads,* with its wonderfully drawn portrait of the goddess), and I do not want to forget to inquire who the author is of "Quester Hero—Myth as Universal Symbol in the Works of Th. M.,"[3] which you mention in the introduction. You do not name him and call the work a manuscript—but it must have been a most interesting one. Has it yet appeared?

I could still speak of our winter journey, to Flanders, England, northern Germany, but *especially* to Flanders, of the winter days in Bruges where we were continually reminded of *The Holy Sinner.* But let us leave that for the propitious hour —and even then, I should rather leave it to my wife—when, after so many years, we hope once more to be permitted to visit you on a hill by the lake that has since become so dear to us too. [. . .]

Auf Wiedersehen, then!

Ever yours,
K. K.

[1.] Vienna, 1953; given as a lecture in Zurich, September 29, 1952, and elsewhere (*GW*, X, 386–399).

[2.] The edition was put out by the Büchergilde Gutenberg (Zurich, 1951). The introduction is "Einführung in den *Zauberberg* für Studenten der Universität Princeton" (*GW*, XI, 602–617).

[3.] Howard Nemerov, "The Quester Hero: Myth as a Universal Symbol in the Works of Thomas Mann," Harvard University thesis, 1940.

Kerényi to Mann

Ponte Brolla, May 2, 1953

Most honored Sir,

Two weeks ago, on my return from Rome, I found the marvelous gift of your volume of essays,[1] and since then it has been a constant source of pleasure to me. And it is a pleasure, furthermore, that one may even conserve this pleasure. One may pause, one *must* in fact, on account of the variety of subject matter, thinking over what has just been read before proceeding to choose—and this too is a pleasure—something new. Your fictional works I can still read only in a state of feverish excitement. But here, in the essays, one has a far greater freedom of enjoyment because, for one thing, the language and the content do not combine to form a single irrepressible current. And one cannot help being astonished over and over again at the manner in which the most varied subjects are fitted to and embodied in the most accomplished, the purest instrument of expression.

[199]

And what magnificient things—verging on the ineffable, like the Hofmannsthal *in memoriam,* or triumphs of critical insight, like the essay on Spengler's thought.[2] The Budapest lecture "Humaniora und Humanismus"[3] provided me, of course, with a deeply moving recollection; I had never read, but only heard it—seventeen years ago. It was only near the end that the recollection actually came to me, in the part that was at the time the most powerful and relevant. It was this that I echoed in my own lecture on humanism and Hellenism[4] during the summer course at the university in Debrecen [Hungary], the lecture that attracted a crowd of visiting German students and subsequently gave me a certain fame in the international press. This is what brought me to the attention of my first nonscholarly publisher, who did so much to bring *Apollon* into existence.

But there is one thought that I overlooked at the time, or else I did not take it in consciously and have remained unconscious of it since, though it could well stand as the motto of the path I have chosen since 1936, the path, namely, that led me out of the purely scholarly field. I read it now, yet more deeply moved and delighted, in the striking formulation at the beginning of your lecture: "Eternal is the universe of things that are never expressed unless they are well expressed." *Utinam!* [Would that it were!]

This represents the standard we have unconsciously followed in our correspondence. Since its publication I have become increasingly convinced of its pedagogic significance; it would really be a shame if at least your part of the exchange did not achieve its educational aim for the largest possible public, since only a small circle could be reached while the letters were being written or at the time of the initial publication. This seems to me the immense significance of all that has been so impressively brought to life again in all "the old and the new,"[5] and that comes to us as a gift: its absolute value as an educational force.

All this, of course, is also to be considered in connection with Dr. [Oskar] Jancke's suggestion, though I, at least, am definitely of two minds. One should keep silent before the public unless one is sure that one will express *it*—what needs to be said—well, and yet one should (although one is very unsure) still attempt it for educational reasons. When he revealed his plan to me in Stuttgart I did not want to spoil what appeared to me his genuine pedagogic zeal, and I naturally kept to my agreement in principle; but I was incapable of conceiving (which I also told him at the time) what would serve for a public dialogue and what—in formal terms—could be made of it. I still feel divided and entrust myself wholly to your instinct and expertise. Nothing can go wrong—I tell myself—where you cheerfully take the lead. In any case, I do not want to be a spoilsport. Plato calls his dialogue about the laws a prudent sport for old men—παιδιὰν παίζειν πρεσβυτικὴν σώφρονα. Thus, the decision is yours.[6]

Ever yours,

K. K.

1. *Altes und Neues: Kleine Prosa aus fünf Jahrzenten* (Frankfort on the Main, 1953).

[2.] "In memoriam Hugo von Hofmannsthal" (*GW*, X, 453–458); "Über die Lehre Spenglers" (*GW*, X, 172–180).

[3.] "Humanistic Studies and Humanism" (*GW*, X, 339–348). An earlier version was delivered in Budapest at a meeting of the Comité International pour la Coopération Intellectuelle of the League of Nations, June 8–12, 1936. In spite of the presence of Fascist delegates, Mann made an extemporaneous attack on the Nazi regime in the course of this meeting (see "Sechzehn Jahre," *GW*, XI, 674 f.)

4. Published in *Apollon*.

[5.] A reference to *Altes und Neues*.

6. The radio program (apparently Dr. Jancke's suggestion) never materialized.

Mann to Kerényi

Erlenbach-Zurich
July 18, 1953

Dear Professor Kerényi,

Moni[1] brought me your excellent book.[2] Warm thanks! I read in it often and find it most enlivening. It could, after all, also be called "Altes und Neues," and the old is distinctly enhanced by the new; for the latter throws new light on the former, which allows it to emerge at last wholly in its own proper light. There is something *heartening* about it all that I find difficult to put into words. And I cannot afford too many words; I am too deeply immersed in my work. We look forward to seeing you and your kind wife in September. We plan a visit to Tessin then and have already reserved rooms at the Villa Castagnola.

Word of my affinity for the mythical, which is actually your discovery, seems by now to have spread. A certain Ernst Alfred Philippson of the University of Illinois (do you know him?) has just sent me an extensive work, *Die Genealogie der Götter in Germanischer Religion, Mythologie und Theologie* [Urbana, Ill., 1953]—which in his terms signify the three levels of the numinous, the poetic, and the systematic-dogmatic. He dedicated it "To the creative narrator of old myths, with deep repect." Perhaps he has learned from you that, while "scholarship must defend its domain from all charlatanism," it is to its advantage to establish friendly relations with the "animating spirit."

Yours,
Thomas Mann

[1.] Probably Monika Mann-Lányi, one of Mann's daughters.
2. *Stunden in Griechenland* (Zurich, 1952) (*ASM*).

[202]

Mann to Kerényi

Dear Professor Kerényi,

Here we are, not far from you, but I find myself—forgive me!—so little inclined to venture out, yet would be so glad to see you and your kind wife. My wife and I would like to ask whether you could come and have lunch with us on Tuesday the 22d or Wednesday the 23d—whichever suits you best—at about 1:00. Philemon and Baucis[2] would be most delighted.

Yours,
Thomas Mann

1. A postcard from the Hotel Villa Castagnola, Lugano.
[2.] An aged couple in Goethe's *Faust*, Part II, Act V.

Kerényi to Mann

Rome, September 25, 1953[1]

Dear, most honored Sir,

For the first time we find ourselves much dismayed to be in *Rome* instead of in Lugano. We have been here since the 20th; thus our regrettable silence. How gladly we would have come! We shall be in Ponte Brolla again after October 6. Perhaps you will still be in Lugano; otherwise perhaps we can make this up at some later time.

Most sincerely,
K. K.

1. A postcard with the Piranesi etching of the Cestius pyramid.

Kerényi to Mann

Ponte Brolla, October 7, 1953

Dear, most honored Sir,

On our return from Rome Saturday we found ourselves the fortunate possessors of *The Black Swan* [1953], already familiar to us from the *Merkur*[1] although it had not yet become one of our intimate possessions. Our thanks are no less warm, though they must be briefer than usual. And haven't you already anticipated in your own dedication all that could be said in a letter of thanks! The thought already came to me when I read the beginning in the *Merkur:* if not "mythos," much less "mythologem," it is still something similar concerning Mother Nature, and not the first instance of that among the writings (and sketches) of Thomas Mann[2]—and now you yourself speak of "myth." Indeed! But I have shot my arrow, and there is nothing to follow except some pedantic question like "Why call such a throbbing, vital contemporary tale a myth?" I am just looking at three butterflies playing in the autumn sun, which has been so late in coming here—not a myth of which even the teller is a part, *only* Mother Nature at play.

I wonder whether you are still in Lugano or in Erlenbach? We continue to regret what we were forced to miss. [. . .]

Let me express our deepest gratitude and devotion.

K. K. and M. K. [Magda Kerényi][3]

[1.] The tale was published in three installments in *Merkur,* 7 (1953).
[2.] See Introduction, note 32, and Mann to Kerényi, August 2, 1947.
[3.] Kerényi's wife.

Mann to Kerényi

Dear Dr. Kerényi,

A thousand thanks for your new work![1] You always have
something interesting and instructive, something exceptionally
stimulating to me personally. Your account of the dissolution
of that intimate link between the divine and history that is implicit in the older mythology is most convincing.

As it happens, I am just now involved (belatedly) with
[Marguerite] Yourcenar's *Memoirs of Hadrian* [1951], an
erudite artistic composition that has delighted me more than
anything else for a long time, and thus I cannot altogether
agree with your closing statement that the insane emperors
and tyrants who, as agents of history, wanted to be gods had
nothing more to do with the divine. I believe, though, that
Hadrian, who was not a bit insane, felt himself to be "divus"
[divine], not only in a figurative sense, but quite seriously as a
god and universal ruler, and even in the deification of his
Bithynian Ganymede he took himself wholly for Jupiter. Certainly, only a stately, wise, and knowing game; but one cannot say that it had nothing more to do with the divine.

Oh, there come times when I feel strongly attracted to your
sphere, and I often long to return to it. I have long since grown
tired of writing the *Confessions of Felix Krull*. Enough of the
manuscript is ready, as a start, so that I can break off a
Part I. If anyone finds these jests too unworthy of my years,
I shall yet begin something completely different. I always come
back to the idea of completing Goethe's *Achilleis* in the form

[205]

of a novel, following his own psychological intentions. I would not have to look far for an adviser for such a project . . .

In fact, my health has given me much concern recently. [. . .] Furthermore, we are forced to stay here on account of affairs related to the imminent purchase of a house—though we have for a long time already wanted to go south. Hopefully, we shall be able to travel by the end of the month, but not farther than Sicily.

Best regards!

Yours,
Thomas Mann

1. "Die Götter und die Weltgeschichte," *Merkur,* 7 (1953), 1097–1108.

Kerényi to Mann

Ponte Brolla, January 26, 1954

Dear, most honored Sir,

Your letter with its exciting hint of a possible, an imminent *Achilleis* from your hands reached me a day before our departure from Rome. I have Goethe's words before me now: "The Achilles tale is a tragic subject, but in view of its singular breadth an epic treatment would not be inappropriate. It is distinctly sentimental and, in view of this dual characteristic, would be well suited for a modern work; a wholly realistic treatment would bring these two inner characteristics into balance. Furthermore, the subject involves a purely personal and private concern, whereas the *Iliad* . . . "[1] Assuredly something for you! And if I could be of service to you, I would gladly put before everything else the gathering of material for the chapter on Achilles in my mythology of the Greek heroes!

But you yourself are already undertaking preparations by familiarizing yourself with the Greek coast of Italy and Sicily —if I understood you correctly—where Goethe found the landscape that aided his understanding of the *Odyssey* and his work on *Nausikaa*. In that case Paestum should not be missed, if possible, particularly the new museum there with the archaic metope reliefs from the temple of Hera at the mouth of the Sele depicting battles and adventures of the heroes. When I hear of such newly excavated finds in the south, I always think regretfully, "Why can't one inform Goethe of this?" But if you go there, I shall feel to some degree consoled. But only to a degree, for I would naturally also like to be present, which would be impossible in February—at the earliest, March or even later.

I must acknowledge, of course, that in connection with such figures as the tortoise rider on a metope, for which there is no parallel in any Greek literary text, I always think of the great epic form, not of psychology. I associate Yourcenar much more with psychology. What visions of power this woman had, who felt impelled to achieve self-realization through such a vivid portrait of a Roman emperor! When, in a single sentence, I alluded to the insane emperors and tyrants who, as agents of history, also wanted to be gods, I thought not of Hadrian but of the type represented by Caligula. Hadrian, on the other hand, I honor for that human and humane poem on the soul:

> Animula vagula blandula
> hospes comesque corporis
> quae nunc abibis in loca
> pallidula rigida nudula
> nec ut soles dabis iocos . . . [2]

It is here that he assumes a place in the history of the true religion of antiquity, with this exquisite instance of a spontaneous relation to being (and what else is *religio* than this), and not where he plays the god-king. How greatly did he challenge Nemesis in this, for such play transgressed the very laws that prescribed man's sphere of being! *It* will claim vengeance—and this is what Nemesis signifies—but the wise man is careful to honor the gods who sway above him in the spheres of being. Thus, at least, if one follows Pindar: "Seek not to become Zeus!"

This in haste on my return home yesterday, to wish you well on your voyage south. For me, alas, the trips north will now resume.

Ever yours,
K. K.

[1.] Goethe to Schiller, May 16, 1798, in *Goethes Briefe,* ed. Karl Robert Mandelkow (Hamburg, 1964), II, 346.

[2.]   Dear fleeting, sweeting, little soul,
    My body's comrade and its guest,
    What region now must be thy goal,
    Poor little wan, numb, naked soul,
    Unable, as of old, to jest?
                [*Minor Latin Poets,* trans. J. W. and A. M. Duff, Loeb Classical Library (Cambridge, Mass.: Harvard University Press, 1961), p. 445]

Mann to Kerényi

February 19, 1954[1]

Dear Professor,

Thanks and greetings! Your "Ekloe"[2] is most suitable for reading in this spot. It is still, after all, the Ionian Sea that one views, even if it is wrapped in rain and mist. Fell ill very soon here, in fact: fever and bronchitis, which were suppressed quickly, perhaps too quickly, with much penicillin! We are still going for a few days to Rome, then to Fiesole, and intend to be back home at the beginning of March.

Yours,

Thomas Mann

1. A postcard from Taormina, Sicily.
2. In *Symbolae Osloenses*, 30 (1953), 82–91.

Kerényi to Mann

Ponte Brolla, October 13, 1954

Dear, most honored Sir,

I can't help anticipating—the publisher will undoubtedly send you *Der göttliche Schelm* as soon as it is ready and properly bound—but I am sending ahead my part of the work,[1] which I think may give you pleasure just at this time, and I include with it the translated Indian text. [. . .]

What concerns me much more is another publication that is due to appear at about the same time as *Der göttliche Schelm* (at Christmas).[2] Perhaps it is not right to bring out something personal and intimate like this while I am still at work on much else—above all, the continuation of my mythological project, *The Heroes of the Greeks*. But should one resign oneself to withholding (for it could not quite find a place in the scholarly work) what one still possesses, without any personal merit, of an older European culture? Doesn't the reality that is called Europe still live only in and through us, particularly through those who, for various reasons, have renounced a "fatherland" in the restricted sense?

I am therefore also sending what is ready of this personal work, especially since it involves an older question, one which I would gladly answer for the reader in the index of this small book. In any case, the preface gives my reasons quite directly. I wonder whether they will gain the approbation of those I value most? I am not presumptuous enough to be altogether sure.

Ever yours,
K. K.

1. C. G. Jung, Karl Kerényi, and Paul Radin, *Der göttliche Schelm: Ein indianischer Mythen-Zyklus* (Zurich, 1954), pp. 155–181 (*The Trickster: A Study in American Indian Mythology* [New York, 1956]).

2. *Unwillkürliche Kunstreisen: Fahrten im alten Europa, 1952–1953* Albae Vigiliae, N.S. XIII–XIV (Zurich, 1954) (*ASM*).

Mann to Kerényi

Kilchberg, [Switzerland], October 17, 1954

Dear Professor,

A thousand thanks for the exciting things you sent.[1] What a remarkable coincidence that the appearance of this book comes at the same time as that of the book [*Confessions of Felix Krull, Confidence Man: The Early Years*] I was in any case about to send you, but which I now hasten to link (though it is quite naturally linked already) to the volume on the primal and essential thief, and especially to your mythological contribution. I was not aware, God knows, of undertaking a Hermetic novel when I began with this forty years ago. I had no other intention than yet another impersonation and parody of art and the artist. It was only in the course of the subsequent continuation that certain associations, undoubtedly induced by the proximity of the *Joseph,* found their way in, and the name of the god arose.

Your introduction is worth its weight in gold, to me at least, and no less so the very poetical *Unwillkürliche Kunstreisen,*

[210]

in which you speak of *The Magic Mountain* and of our correspondence. It has been a remarkable thing, this relationship of ours! After the *Joseph,* I thought to myself: "Yes, certainly, that was an interesting and productive episode, the exchange with that scholar. Now we are probably fairly well finished with one another, and our ways will presumably separate." Not at all! Nothing of an episode. It seems that in spite of the differences in our modes of expression, our spheres will repeatedly come into contact; and what is to me (and probably to you too) an increasingly striking proximity and parallelism of interests and of intellectual orientation has come to the surface, a phenomenon of predestined friendship to which, for all its strangeness, we acquiesce most happily.

The author of that work on the Quester hero is Howard Nemerov.[2] [. . .]

Yours,
Thomas Mann

1. See Kerényi to Mann, October 13, 1954, notes 1 and 2.
[2.] See Kerényi to Mann, February 17, 1953.

Kerényi to Mann

Ponte Brolla, October 26, 1954

Dear, most honored Sir,

At this hour, on concluding *The Early Years,* let me convey to you, together with my thanks for your present of this singular book[1]—or perhaps *as* thanks—at least this one observation that came to me in the course of reading, a culminating thought that coincides with the culmination of the book, a moment of heightened insight in which you have every right to take part.

Here I come again into that sphere where we are "predestined" (as you put it) sojourners, a sphere that has determined our contact from the start, setting it apart, irrespective of many other hours of association, as a friendship "not of this world." This is the sphere of the daimonic, which I spell in the Greek manner to distinguish it from the demonic, although the unconscious-creative sphere I mean (where "unconscious" is only meant to indicate the deep-rooted aspect of the creative) also has much to do with the demonic, notably where it fuses with Christianity in its historical phase (not with Christ, who was anchored in the daimonic). Let us then leave spelling aside, or save it for a special "investigation." The artistic composition is clearly enough manifested in that the *corrida* [bullfight] comes prior to the climax, the utterly unexpected, unsurpassable "Holé! Heho! Ahé!" of the great Iberian mother.[2] This is daimonic-demonic—as you wish.

For Professor Kuckuck well knows, and Krull babbles after him, that the bullfight, said to represent the great sacrifice in honor of Mithras, the god of a secret military brotherhood, is in essence *just that*. This theory you put forward (thank God, I am tempted to say, in view of the surprise your daimon has in store for us). But I do not believe that *this* explanation (and I know others, even a "philosophical" one) of the religious significance of a *corrida* can be based wholly on a scholarly theory. At this point art, the daimon, takes over—in consequence of an insight (I do not know this, but assume it) that transcends *every* insight, looking toward the primordial source.

But what in this instance is primordial? Certainly not *merely* the *taurobolai*[3] or *only* the honor given the soldiers' god Mithras! The sacrifice of bulls in the distinctive form we find in the bullfights of the Iberian Peninsula is surely not just something imported by the Roman army from Persia; it represents an ancient Mediterranean inheritance. It already existed in ancient Crete, where youths jumped in breathtaking fashion around and on top of the holy beast—in honor of the Great

[212]

Mother. It is in *her* honor that the bull is killed (and killed in just that manner). If one speaks purely in terms of art history, the model for Mithras as slayer of bulls (a Hellenistic creation) is *Nike* as slayer of bulls, found in Attic illustrations—the representative of a mightier and more ancient goddess.

Who *triumphs* in your *corrida* if not she who exclaims, "Holé! Heho! Ahé!"? How magnificent, how well planned in terms of religious history! Planned? You know best whether this was planned or "merely" composed, *artistically,* to lead to the "mighty outcry"—whose? May I be permitted to respond to this jest with a delight that goes beyond a naïve burst of laughter?

Ever yours,
K. K.

1. *Bekenntnisse des Hochstaplers Felix Krull: Der Memoiren erster Teil* (Frankfort on the Main, 1954) (*Confessions of Felix Krull, Confidence Man: The Early Years,* trans. D. Lindley [New York, 1955]). Mann's inscription cited a Flaubert passage from my contribution to *Der göttliche Schelm* (*The Trickster*) in order to "link" the two books.

Translator's note: The inscription, reproduced in facsimile in the German edition, is:

" . . . ça finissait par n'être plus indécent. Il y en a plusieurs, Carragheuss . . . Il s'agit seulement de montrer le plus possible de phallus. Le plus grand avait un grelot qui, à chaque mouvement de reins, sonnait; *cela faisait beaucoup de rire.*"

[" . . . in the end it was no longer indecent. There were a number of them, these Carragheuss. . . . The point was to show as much as possible of phallus. The largest had a small bell which, with every movement of the loins, tinkled; *that caused great laughter.*"]

To Karl Kerényi, to whom, as seems fated, I shall remain continually obliged.

Kilchberg, October, 1954

Thomas Mann

The Flaubert passage comes from the notes to his African voyage of 1858 (in *Voyages,* ed. René Dumesnil [2 vols.; Paris, 1948], II, 552).

The Carragheuss figure (also Karagouz and other variants), a hero of traditional Turkish shadow plays, is noted for his foolery and farcical obscenities. See *The Trickster,* p. 184, and E. Littré, *Dictionnaire,* Supplement (Paris, 1881).

[2.] The exclamation is by Maria Pia, Professor Kuckuck's wife, as she embraces Felix at the conclusion of *Felix Krull* (*GW,* VII, 661).

[3.] A Roman ritual of oriental origin in which an initiate is drenched by the blood of a bull.

Kerényi to Mann

Ascona, Casa del Sole, November 8, 1954

Dear, most honored Sir,

As I write you my new address, I ask myself, What will be the next marvel we shall read *here—Krull* II or something else mentioned in an earlier letter? It is the *Heroes of the Greeks* that awaits me urgently; I hope yet to take up the threads this month. The loom is to be found on the [Monte] Gianicolo [in Rome], while the house that has taken us in—but for how long?—is on Monte Verità in Ascona. Returning to this landscape that has become a home to us since 1943 was unexpected even for us—the *Unwillkürliche Kunstreisen* ["Involuntary Art Journeys"] moves further into the past; Ponte Brolla reveals itself as only a way station.

With warmest greetings,

Yours,
K. K.

Mann to Kerényi

Kilchberg am Zürichsee
Alte Landstrasse 39
December 5, 1954

Dear Professor Kerényi,

After receiving from you the "definitive version" of the *Unwillkürliche Kunstreisen* in galley proof, I now also have (together with *Der göttliche Schelm*) the published volume from the Rhein-Verlag, with the lovely carriage of Apollo on the dust jacket and the generous selection of Pompeian and other pictures, some altogether enchanting. Let me congratulate you on this new publication, so alluring and winning, at once light and full of substance. It will be a joy to many readers! I had already read these "excursions in old Europe" in proof and now only leafed through, rereading some parts and looking at the pictures; and two things impressed me strongly: first, why I returned to it, and second, how remarkably the enjoyment of life is elevated, intensified, strengthened, made into a continuing celebration, both spiritual and sensual, by means of the training, the knowledge, the sense of beauty, the joyous and erudite cultivation of the eye. To which, of course, must be added how far behind you I remain in the capacity to partake of such pleasures, because of my scandalous lack of education. Of course, I need not confess like the great Schiller, "Unfortunately, Italy, and particularly Rome, is no country for me; the physical aspects would oppress me and the aesthetic interest would provide no compensation, since I lack both an interest in and an apprehension of the plastic arts."[1] I have a devout and passionate regard for Rome, for its art treasures of thousands of years, for its majestic survey of the whole of our culture, and you are altogether justified in writing that I was "not lacking in due reverence" there, and also that I was overcome as if in a dream to stand in front of *the* Pope.[2] But there does exist a certain troubling affinity between me and that poet [Schiller], who bewailed his ignorance and was inhibited from attempting an epic because he "lacked the skills" a Homeric poet requires. The world of the eyes is not actually my world either, and at heart *I want to see nothing*—just like him. Why didn't he even *once,* before or during the composition of [*Wilhelm*] *Tell,* undertake a brief excursion to Switzerland? It would have been easy to manage. He wanted to see nothing. He planned dramas involving adventures at sea ("Das Schiff," "Die Flibustier") and never had the slightest thought of traveling to the ocean, much less over the ocean. He wanted to derive everything from himself and, by his own account, he constructed a type of drama that corresponded to his requirements, his deficiencies, his possibilities, one in which, consequently, he would "necessarily achieve a certain excellence."[3] How familiar I find this! Thus I have fashioned out of my capacities and my profound incapacities a certain type of novel in which I "necessarily excel." But that I have never gone to Greece! (Except for twenty minutes on the Acropolis and a glance at the studio of Phidias in the museum in Athens.) I wanted to see nothing—or at least to see no more of Greece than could be seen incidentally in Italy.

How well *you* understand traveling! I have no desire at all to travel, because of laziness, lack of experience, because I have too much to do. But you certainly have much to do too, and yet you have made us proud of our old Europe by such a book as this.

Yours,
Thomas Mann

[1.] Schiller to Wilhelm von Humboldt, February 17, 1803; in Friedrich Schiller, *Briefe,* ed. G. Fricke (Munich, 1955), p. 599.

[216]

[2.] See *Unwillkürliche Kunstreisen,* p. 92 (*ASM,* p. 136), where Kerényi gives his impressions of a talk he has had with Mann about Mann's audience with Pope Pius XII in April 1953. For Mann's own account see Thomas Mann, *Briefwechsel mit seinem Verleger Gottfried Bermann Fischer, 1932–1955,* letter of May 27, 1953.

[3.] Schiller, in a letter of February 25, 1789, to Christian Gottfried Körner, wrote, "But what I have actually done is to fashion a drama according to my own talent, one in which I achieve a certain excellence just because it is my own" (*Briefe,* p. 197). Mann quotes the sentence accurately in the long essay *Versuch über Schiller* (Frankfort on the Main, 1955); see *GW,* IX, 945.

Kerényi to Mann

Casa del Sole, Ascona
December 31, 1954

Dear, most honored Sir,

Let this letter serve not only to express my gratitude [. . .] but also to make some unavoidable confessions. *How often* in reading your novels have I felt scandalously uneducated! Did I, for example, know anything of the existence of a Neapolitan humanist called Settembrini (except in *The Magic Mountain*) until, much later, I discovered his writings in a used-book shop on the Campo di Fiori in Rome? Did I know anything of the Jewish hagiographic writings regarding Joseph when I came to your tales? Or the kinds of details about Weimar society that are to be found in *The Beloved Returns,* until I read the novel? Not to mention the musical instruments in *Doctor Faustus* . . .

I could pursue this to linguistic-philological matters in *The Holy Sinner* and *The Black Swan,* and to data on Parisian streets in *Krull*—where, incidentally, one can find the most astonishing and marvelous things about the *eyes,* the eyes of the artist! To which you would naturally reply that in each case you prepared yourself conscientiously for the given field. But that's just it: one must *be able* to immerse oneself in a specific subject! The old, static concept of "education" in terms of factual data is long since outdated; it has, furthermore, revealed its moral insufficiency in not being able to muster, then or now, the slightest power of resistance against the totalitarian assaults of barbarism or sham culture.

What we, old Europeans, can still teach the younger generation is simply and solely what ties together our factually oriented (and thus necessarily limited) education and the kind of receptivity and willingness to learn, both the old and the new, that comes from a feeling for quality born of intimate involvement with specific fields of knowledge. In publishing our correspondence, the *Stunden in Griechenland,* and most recently the *Kunstreisen,* I have always thought of this younger generation, in order to say to it: "Look! This is how we learn, undogmatically and yet not nihilistically, we old ones who embrace the whole range of bygone culture in all possible permutations!" How could we, in our inner being, exist otherwise?

It is in this spirit that I can still send you good wishes for the New Year, which is the intent of this letter and what comes with it,[1] some of which is probably already familiar to you. With regard to *Geistiger Weg Europas* let me note that this lecture focuses on the intellectual situation in the German-speaking part of Europe (in the lecture series the English was represented by Toynbee, the French by Camus); it was given at the invitation of the book dealers' association of The Hague on the occasion of its hundredth anniversary, in one of the medieval halls of the Binnenhof. This event in October was for me the crowning moment of my "excursions in old Europe."

With warmest good wishes,

Yours,
K. K.

1. *Geistiger Weg Europas,* Albae Vigiliae, N.S. XVI (Zurich, 1955).

Kerényi to Mann

Ascona, June 15, 1955

Most honored Sir,

The typing is because I want to impose on you as little as possible: what I need to put before you might not be so clear if I wrote by hand. What is involved is *The Transposed Heads* —the subject of our most recent conversation—and my still partially deficient marginalia to it.[1] I send them to you now in corrected form, cleared of those errors that were further aggravated by the unnecessary meddling of a newspaper copy-reader. All this, of course, is now beside the point, and I can only console myself regarding the essential matter with the thought that something similar befell the great Sanskrit scholar [Theodor] Benfey when he sought to uncover the sources of Goethe's "Legende"[2] in his periodical *Orient und Occident* (1860, 719 ff.): He skipped over the important passage in Sonnerat's *Reise nach Ostindien und China* (1783), which is the source of Goethe's treatment of the exchange of the heads, verifying all sorts of other things of interest and import, only not the crucial point. Subsequently he himself confessed, like the great scholar he was, that this essay was his most faulty effort—which was certainly an exaggeration.

Now I do not want to exaggerate but only to tell you at what point I can go no further without your help. My mistaken assumption was that you took the tale of the transposed heads, which is to be found in various Indian collections of fairy tales, from Hemawidschaja's[3] already parodistic treatment. I am forced now to reject this assumption, a fact that leaves me all the more astonished at the correspondences between your composition and the minor art work of the late Indian storyteller. This, again, represents for me an exceptional spectacle and revelation of intellectual history, and I should like to share my own pleasure with the others—that secret band of true readers.

After our conversation I can no longer assume that you have read, if not Hemawidschaja in [Johannes] Hertel's *Indische Märchen* [Jena, 1919], then at least the *Wetalapantschawinsati, Die Fünfundzwanzig Erzählungen eines Dämons* ["Twenty-Five Tales of a Goblin"] as translated by Heinrich Uhle [Munich, 1924]; or the Persian-Turkish *Tuti-Nameh*, the *Papagaienbuch* [*Tales of a Parrot*] as translated by Iken or [Georg] Rosen; or its source the *Schukasaptati*, the *Siebenzig Erzählungen des Papageis* ["Seventy Tales of a Parrot"] in Richard Schmidt's translation [1899]. In all of these one may find the novella of the transposed heads, not Goethe's legend with the mother of course, but yours, involving a young woman and two men. Furthermore, one also finds there the temple of Devi Kali Durga as the scene of the grisly, comical act, something I had suspected but could not be sure of on the basis of the Hemawidschaja alone.

If one discounts all of these possible sources, all that seems to remain is Heinrich Zimmer's *Maya* [Stuttgart, 1936], which you yourself have cited with praise, both earlier and again in our recent conversation. But here two difficulties present themselves. First of all, I can locate only Zimmer's reference to Goethe's "Legende" and its source (*Maya*, pp. 229 ff.). It is possible that I have overlooked another passage, where he mentions the other legend (and with what sources, I wonder?). This is very well possible; there have been more famous instances in scholarship. But even so, a second difficulty would still remain, which I could only solve by the assumption of a second source, one similar to Hertel's *Indische Märchen*. This also indicates the internal, philological basis for my false assumption.

You utilize, in fact, three different modes of transcribing

Indian names: (1) that of Zimmer in his popular book *Maya,* namely, without marking the vowel length, with "sch" in the German manner and yet with the full Sanskrit root of the masculine in "-a"; (2) the more exact and scholarly method, marking the vowel length and with "sh" in the English manner, as in "Shûdra," "Kâli," "Durgâ"; (3) the orthography of older renderings (including Goethe's), with the modern Hindi synaloepha of the above-mentioned "-a" of the masculine, as in "Schridaman." The coexistence of the last two forms is perfectly conceivable in a collection of fairy tales, in tales drawn from Sanskrit and from modern Hindi texts. Let me add too your most subtle differentiation of "siyât" and "siyâ" —the fruit of perceptive study, as well as an astonishing instance of attunement, of "making contact," to use your own term.

I have been concerned from the start, of course, primarily with the kind of attunement that comes from a creative, spontaneous impulse. Yet this needs to be distinguished, to be cleansed, one might say, from the kind that derives from one's reading experience; and the latter, a rare phenomenon in such an esoteric field, delights me hardly less. It would be senseless to waste much time on this minor philological matter, especially since you can solve it easily by consulting your memory. This is why I have broached it to you before turning to the larger issue.

Let me close in grateful recollection of the rich feast you have provided me.

Yours,
K. K.

1. "Marginalien zu den 'Vertauschten Köpfen,'" *Neue Zürcher Zeitung,* June 5, 1955. The solution of the problem may be found in a revision of this essay: "Die goldene Parodie," *Die Neue Rundschau,* 67 (1956), 549–556.

[2.] A poem of 1824.

[3.] Often spelled Hemavijaya (c. 1565–1631), author of *Kathā-ratnākara;* German translation by Johannes Hertel, *Das Märchenmeer* (Munich, 1920).

Mann to Kerényi

Kilchberg am Zürichsee
Alte Landstrasse 39
June 23, 1955

Dear Dr. Kerényi,

Your new essay in *Studium Generale*[1] has just arrived. I scanned it immediately and admired your spirited literary productivity. It almost appears as if you were forced into it; there is a constant demand of more from you, for the timeliness (one might better say the "timing") of the mythological is *your* timeliness; you have helped to bring it about, and your name rises and rises.

I am so little able to explain to you what may have helped me with *The Transposed Heads!* The sad thing is that I immediately forget the sources on which I draw in composing a work and am barely able to give any account whatever of them. I do recall that, in addition to the *Maya* book, I read all sorts of informative things, notably about Indian temples and the Great Mother, but *no* Indian version of the fable and nothing that anticipated the parodistic spirit of my own treatment.

We fly to Holland on the 30th, taking with us a couple of hundred still unopened birthday letters that we hope to go through and answer in Noordwijk. This dear world has dealt with me in a most boisterous manner. Let me advise you not to carry it too far with fame!

Yours sincerely,
Thomas Mann

[222]

1. "Gedanken über die Zeitmässigkeit einer Darstellung der griechischen Mythologie" ("Thoughts on the Timeliness of a Presentation of the Mythology of Greece"), *Studium Generale,* 8 (1955), 268–272, an essay published after many years' delay. It was originally to be entitled "Prolegomena zu einer Darstellung der griechischen Mythologie" ("Prolegomena to a Presentation of the Mythology of Greece") and was unfortunately very hastily rechristened.

Index

[228]

Plato, 111, 153, 154, 157, 201
Plutarch, *De Iside et Osiride*, 35
Poliziano, Angelo Ambrogini, 130, 132n
Potiphar's wife, 65, 71, 72, 76
Powys, J. C., 189, 192; *Glastonbury Romance, A,* 8, 35, 44; *In Defense of Sensuality,* 37; *Meaning of Culture, The,* 37; *Wolf Solent,* 42
Priapus, 44
"Primordial Child in Primordial Times, The" (Kerényi), 98-99n, 100
Princeton, N.J., 81-82, 90, 95
"Problem der Freiheit, Das" (Mann), 150n
Prometheus (Kerényi), 86, 87n, 131, 139, 140n, 181n
Psychology, 28, 100, 103

Ravensbrück concentration camp, 131, 135
"Religio Academici" (Kerényi), 77n-78n
Religion, 16, 20; history of, 7, 11, 33, 34, 36-37, 40, 48-49, 52; secularization of, 74-76
Religione antica, La (Kerényi), 78n, 99
Religion of the Greeks and Romans, The (Kerényi), 16n, 29n, 77n, 80n, 99n, 100n
"Religiöse Idee des Nichtseins, Die" (Kerényi), 80n
Rhodes, 63
Rivista di filologia classica, 60
Romandichtung und Mythologie, xiii, 122, 124n
Rome, 131, 137-138, 149, 167, 170, 189, 203, 206
Rosenberg, Alfred, 102n
Rychner, Max, 137, 139n

Satire, 49, 53
"Satire und Satura" (Kerényi), 49, 50n, 53
Savonarola, Girolamo, 23, 130, 132n

Schiefner, Anton, 94
Schiller, J. C. F. von, 215-216, 217n
Schönberg, Arnold, 177n
Schopenhauer, Arthur, 67, 82, 127, 151
Schweizerische Musikzeitung, 171
Settembrini, 7, 13, 39, 44, 130, 217
Sketch of My Life, A (Mann), 18-19n
Socrates, 35, 131, 159
Sophocles, "Hunters" ("Ichneutae"), 52, 54n
Sophron, 49, 60, 67, 78
"Sophron oder der griechische Naturalismus" (Kerényi), 60n, 79n
Sörensen, Bengt Algot, 10, 20-22
Spitteler, Carl, 119; *Olympischer Frühling,* 121n-122n
Storm, Theodor, 62
Story of a Novel, The (Mann), ix, 177n
Studium Generale, 222
Stunden in Griechenland (Kerényi), 202n
Switzerland, 59, 84, 87, 104, 117, 129-131, 139, 158, 166, 168, 181, 183, 189, 198, 216
Szondi, Leopold, 104, 171

Tables of the Law, The (Mann), 23, 28, 107, 118, 120-121
Tales of Jacob, The (Mann), see under *Joseph and His Brothers*
Tat, 137
Telesphoros, 38, 39n, 173
"Telesphoros" (Kerényi), 36n
Tessin, Switzerland, xii, 109, 120, 125, 138, 166, 167, 196, 202
This Peace (Mann), 84, 85n, 87
"Thomas Mann und der Teufel in Palestrina" (Kerényi), 177n
Thucydides, 110
"Titanismus und Humanismus in der griechischen Mythologie" (Kerényi), 197n
Töchter der Sonne (Kerényi), 19, 29, 108n, 109, 114n, 127n

[230]

Mythology and Humanism

Designed by R. E. Rosenbaum.
Composed by York Composition Co., Inc.,
in 11 point Intertype Baskerville, 2 points leaded,
with display lines in monotype Baskerville.
Printed letterpress from type by York Composition Co., Inc.,
on Warren's No. 66 text, 50 pound basis,
with the Cornell University Press watermark.
Bound by Vail-Ballou Press
in Columbia book cloth
and stamped in All Purpose foil.